CENTRE FOR THE STUDY OF ISLAM AND OTHER FAITHS

CSIOF Bulletin

Issue No. 6/7
2013 - 2014

CSIOF Bulletin
No 6. (2013 - 2014)
ISBN-10:0992476321
ISBN-13:978-0-9924763-2-8

© 2014 Melbourne School of Theology Press. All rights reserved.

Editor
Ruth Nicholls

Assistant Editor
Liz Burley

Production and Cover Design
Ho-yuin Chan

Publishing Services
Published by MST Press
Thank you to Richard Shumack for his publishing services.

Centre for the Study of Islam and Other Faiths
Melbourne School of Theology
5 Burwood Highway, Wantirna, Victoria 3152, Australia.
PO Box 6257, Vermont Sth, Victoria 3133, Australia
Ph: +61 3 9881 7800, Fax: +61 3 9800 0121
csiof@mst.edu.au, www.mst.edu.au/csiof

People involved in Christian interface with other religions are welcome to submit related articles to the Editor for consideration for publishing in the CSIOF Bulletin.

Opinions and conclusions published in the CSIOF Bulletin are those of the authors and do not necessarily represent the views of the CSIOF or its Editors. The Bulletin is purely an information medium, to inform interested parties of religious trends, discussions and debates. The Bulletin affirms the free expression of the religious convictions of its authors but rejects hatred towards any persons or religious group

EDITORIAL — 5
FEATURES — 7

Limiting religious freedom in Australia — 7
Hindutva — 19
Was Allah testing Zia-ul-Haq? — 26
Ahmadis:
A Minority in the Context of Pakistan — 29
Honour Crimes — 36
Building Bridges through Stories — 46
Oh Christians, Leave our Lands! — 58
Shari'a Finance Uncovered — 61

COMMUNIQUÉS — 64

Allah, God, and the Trouble with Language — 64
Egypt's Revolution II (July 2013) — 70
The Church's R2P — 74
The Legacy of the Mughals — 76
Christian-Muslim Relations — 80
Tomé Pires — 82
Australia:
The Changing Religious Profile Down Under — 90

REFLECTIONS — 93

Islamic "Peace Conference" in Melbourne — 93
Ministry to Muslim Women — 95
Zorro, Goldilocks and Jesus — 101
Sharing Christianity with Muslims — 103
'Talking Past Each Other': — 105

REVIEWS — 108

The Makings of Indonesian Islam: — 108
Islam and Christianity on the Edge — 114
Islam and Christianity on the Edge — 116
Turn Back the Battle — 118

The Wisdom of Islam and the Foolishness of Christianity   120

CSIOF NEWS AND ACTIVITIES   122

Notes for Contributors   125

Editorial

Yes, this is a combined 2013-2014 edition of the CSIOF Bulletin. A number of factors have contributed to the delay in printing the 2013 edition, so it was decided to make it a combined 2013-2014 production. In the future the nature of the Bulletin may change as well as possibly being available electronically for in essence production processes and costs have been part of the issues involved.

The articles in this edition of the Bulletin reflect the dual thrust of the Centre for the Study of Islam and Other Faiths: the study of Islam (the majority of articles) and two concerning other Faiths. The two articles on other Faiths emanate from the Indian context. One takes the reader into the world of the Sikhs while the other outlines the rise of the Hindu fundamentalist party and its success in the recent elections.

The topics dealing with Islamic issues invite thoughtful consideration especially in light of the recent developments in the Middle East that have followed on from the Arab Spring of 2010. What will the future bring? This is a question that most thinking people, whether Christian, Muslim or Hindu, find breaking into their conscious thinking. Some, like the Kuwaiti journalist whose article has been included, are expressing their despair, confusion and a sense of bewilderment. From a different perspective Qaiser Julius writes of the plight of the Ahmadis, a group who consider themselves Muslims but have no rights and no place within the context of the Islamic country in which they sought a home. Indirectly Qaiser raises the question of religious freedom which is the subject of PC's article which assesses some poignant issues relating to the question. What does religious freedom really mean especially when religion and politics are closely intertwined? How can religious freedom operate in a world where that freedom has different meanings? It is questions such as these that also underlie the issues of Shari'a finance. Even the article on Zia ul Haq raises issues of religion and politics and its consequences.

More recently, the beheading of the Western hostages, even if they have adopted Islam has hit the headlines. Less frequently but equally disturbing are the reports in the media of family members threating to kill a female relative in the name of 'honour' and even more concerning are the actual accounts of 'honour crimes.' Amelia Gibson explores this practice of 'honour killings' in her article, while seeking to find a Christian response.

The relationship of the word *Allah* and God, especially as used by Christians, is a contentious issue. Neely's article provides very helpful insights into the issue and perhaps will even have the reader evaluating his/her own use of the word 'god' especially in a multicultural environment. Over recent years, the importance and significance of story-telling has been increasingly scrutinised by many disciplines and is being profitably used in a wide variety of situations and for varying purposes. Not surprisingly, many are revisiting the role of story in the proclamation of the Good News. After all, much of the Old Testament is story and Jesus Christ himself was a master storyteller. Macy Wong examines the role of storytelling in engaging others in considering the claims and teaching of the Gospel.

As with every issue of the Bulletin, book reviews fill an important role of providing insights into the publications now available. In this issue the books reviewed are well worth consideration. For those following the growth of Islam especially in Asia, *The Makings of Indonesian Islam* by Laffan should be of interest. For a philosophical and apologetic approach to Islam then take time to read the review of Shumack's *The Wisdom of Islam and the Foolishness of Christianity*. If on the other hand, your interests are more eclectic and wider in scope then *Islam and Christianity on the Edge* would provide you with some interesting and thoughtful reading. Elizabeth Kendal's book *Turn Back the Battle* is perhaps a more disturbing book for she has assumed a more prophetic role which for some may be somewhat challenging.

So as the Editor I trust that you the reader will find something to interest you, something to challenge you and even something you want to question and query. Don't hesitate to contact us for it is only as the Bulletin serves your interests that it will survive.

Ruth Nicholls

Features

Limiting religious freedom in Australia
A discussion in relation to one of the minority faiths

PC*
Student

Melbourne School of Theology

Introduction

Religious diversity in Australia is increasing as a result of the global movement of people and ideas. The interconnectedness of the global community has meant that our community engages one another's religion not in principle and theory but increasingly in practice. Since religious pluralism is now a practical reality of everyday life in our multicultural society, religious freedom is a consequential issue of today.

Since the dismantling of the 'White Australia' policy, successive migrant intakes have considerably diversified the Australian population. This has resulted in the growth and arrival of new religious traditions[1], making the religious profile of Australia partly Christian, multi-faith and secularist.

In our democratic society, religious freedom is necessary but complex as considerations of individual rights and public interests are taken into account. This discussion will begin by highlighting the importance of religious freedom. Then the appraisal will turn to address the need for limits to religious freedom.

> *In our democratic society, religious freedom is necessary but complex as considerations of individual rights and public interests are taken into account.*

---

*PC is a pseudonym.

[1] These traditions include Buddhist, Confucian, Hindu, and Humanist, Islamic, Sikh and Taoist traditions. G. Bouma, D. Cahill, H. Dellal, A. Zwartz, *Freedom of Religion and Belief in the 21st century Australia* (Australian Human Rights Commission, 2011), 4

Furthermore, the paper will propose principles in determining the limitations set for the minority faith of Islam.

Religious Freedom - A Fundamental Human Right
The freedom of religion and belief is recognized as a fundamental human right in the *Universal Declaration of Human Rights,* as 'a common standard of achievement for all peoples and all nations'[2]. The Australian Government has also ratified the *International Covenant on Civil and Political Rights* in 1980[3] which guarantees in the clearest and strongest terms the need to protect this fundamental right.

Parkinson[4] defines religious freedom by following five basic freedoms implicit within those rights. These freedoms are:
- Freedom to manifest a religion through religious observance and practice
- Freedom to appoint people of faith to organizations run by faith communities
- Freedom to teach and uphold moral standards within faith communities
- Freedom of conscience to discriminate between right and wrong
- Freedom to teach and persuade others.

---

[2] Article 18: 1 states: "Everyone has the right to freedom of thought, conscience and religion; this right includes freedom to change his religion or belief, and freedom, either alone or in community with others and in public or private, to manifest his religion or belief in teaching, practice, worship and observance." This was proclaimed by the United Nations in 1946. Bouma, *Freedom of Religion*, 2-3

[3] Article 18 of the Covenant states:
1. Everyone shall have the right to freedom of thought, conscience and religion. This right shall include freedom to have or to adopt a religion or belief of his choice and freedom, either individually or in community with others and in public or private, to manifest his religion or belief in worship, observance, practice and teaching.
2. No one shall be subject to coercion which would impair his freedom to have or to adopt a religion or belief of his choice.
3. Freedom to manifest one's religion or beliefs may be subject only to such limitations as are prescribed by law and are necessary to protect public safety, order, health or morals or the fundamental rights and freedoms of others.

The States Parties to the present Covenant undertake to have respect for the liberty of parents and, when applicable, legal guardians to ensure the religious and moral education of their children in conformity to their own convictions. Bouma, *Freedom of Religion*, 3

[4] P. Parkinson, *National Agenda For Religious Freedom*, (http://www.ea.org.au/site/DefaultSite/filesystem/documents/public%20policy/A%20NATIONAL%20AGENDA%20FOR%20RELIGIOUS%20FREEDOM.pdf cited May 2014), 1

While religious diversity is accepted and viewed as a positive value for society, people of faith have rising concerns about threats to religious freedom in Australia, both at personal and state/federal levels. These concerns derive from issues surrounding hostile attitudes towards religious beliefs by the growing secular community, the uncritical attempt to provide equal rights to minority faiths, the antithetical beliefs of differing religions, the difficult balance between personal rights and public interest and the potential conflicts between the freedom of religion and other freedoms (e.g. discrimination and speech). These concerns pose a challenge of how these rights can be integrated so that all religions in Australia would benefit from the protection of religious freedom.

Exposing Underlying Assumptions about Religious Freedom
Before attempting to determine how these rights are to be protected, it is important to critically expose underlying assumptions that can hinder our attempts to maintain true religious freedom:

Religion is a private matter and not for the public square
The growing secularist voice within Australia has insisted their right to freedom **from** religion. In an attempt to maintain their 'freedom' there has been a push to confine religion to the private sphere as religious values were not considered relevant in a plural society. However this is impossible as religion inevitably has significantly shaped social policies within Australia[5].

Tolerance is about offence
Tolerance has been embraced as the 'Australian way' in an attempt to foster social cohesion in our multicultural society[6]. However tolerance can breed ignorance if it becomes uncritical tolerance. Carson identifies a shift in our understanding of the old tolerance to the new tolerance from defending the rights of those who

> *... religious freedom is truly protected for the public good when tolerance is practiced among those holding differing beliefs for the purpose of discerning what is truth, rather than censoring truth to avoid the risk of offence.*

---

[5] G. Bouma, 'Religious Diversity and Social Policy: An Australian Dilemma' (AJSI, 47/3, 2012), 282

[6] S Parkinson, 'The Australian Immigration Book' (Cremorne Junction, NSW: Made to Measure Publications, 2014), 28

hold different beliefs to affirming all beliefs as equally valid. "This new tolerance sacrifices wisdom and principle in support of one supreme good: upholding their view of tolerance and those who uphold and practice the older tolerance, are written off as intolerant"[7]. Such a shift runs the risk of morphing tolerance from an issue of truth into an issue of offense. Hence religious freedom is truly protected for the public good when tolerance is practiced among those holding differing beliefs for the purpose of discerning what is truth, rather than censoring truth to avoid the risk of offence.

Providing equal opportunity to all religions will result in mutual benefit

The challenge of religious freedom is giving an equal voice to majority and minority religious communities. Often minority communities can lack the capacity to reply to criticism hence find themselves in a position that can amount to a sense of implicit rejection[8]. However, there can be a high level of concern that there is too much deference to religious minorities, especially the Muslim communities, at the expense of mainstream values[9] There is a false assumption that all religions are the same and providing equal opportunity will result in the wider public interest. It is important that we identify the distinctiveness of each religion in the public square based on an objective assessment of a religion's ideology in the sacred texts and its ideal model of faith and provide 'opportunity' accordingly. Such critical assessments will empower us to see if our current practice in the name of 'equal opportunity' will actually lead to the equal benefit of society.

> *There is a false assumption that all religions are the same and providing equal opportunity will result in the wider public interest.*

It's important to expose such assumptions so that we are conscious of its influence on policies and we can critically and wisely foster

---

[7] D. A. Carson, *The Intolerance of Tolerance* (Grand Rapids, Michigan: W. B. Eerdmans Publishing Company, 2012), 98

[8] Bouma, *Freedom of Religion*, 24

[9] Bouma, *Freedom of Religion*, 23

personal religious freedom but not at the expense of the public safety.

The Need for Limits to Religious Freedom

"Freedom to manifest one's religion or beliefs may be subject only to such limitations as are prescribed by law and are necessary to protect public safety, order, health or morals or the fundamental rights and freedoms of others." [10]

The religious freedom that underpins our democracy does not privilege individual belief above all else. The challenge is that there is no legitimate, standardized public test for an individual's religious beliefs. How do we know what's sincere and what's opportunistic? Who is the judge? How does this not devolve into a broad excuse for law breaking or the kind of excessive entanglement of legitimizing religious prejudice with government? While every individual may lay claim to their personal rights, there is need for limits through laws and social policies to religious freedom. These hold individuals to account for their personal responsibility to the public interest and to protect the public from religious and personal excesses.

Bouma distinguishes four ways religion relates to public and social policy: religion as the subject, source, critic and implementer of social policies[11]. As such the impact of religious expression in the public square is significant ranging from freedoms of speech and discrimination, ethos (exemptions, employment, service provision), legislation (constitutional, national, state based), government and diversity (the role of government in diversity and religious diversity), education (religion in governmental schools) and health[12]. Given this broad impact, it is important to recognize that different considerations are needed when setting limits to religious freedom at a personal compared to a state/federal level.

The Challenges of Religious Freedom for a Muslim

---

[10] Article 18 International Covenant on Civil and Political Rights. Bouma, *Freedom of Religion*, 3

[11] Bouma, *Australian Soul - Religion and Spirituality in the Twenty-first Century*, (Melbourne, VIC., Cambridge University Press 2006), 176

[12] Bouma, *Freedom of Religion*, 30-58

Muslims in Australia have grown over the years to represent 2.2% of the Australian population[13]. Since the September 11 attacks, it has stirred a sense of Islamophobia among Westerners. As such there are challenges that Muslims migrants face in being unfairly stereotyped and discriminated against. In addition, their integration into western society confronts them with a risk of their religious practices merging into Australian culture. This leads to alternations in religious practices, such that these practices are less external and visible and more internal and personal, particularly among young people[14].

FAIR (Forum on Australia's Islamic Relations) wrote that "... on a day to day level, there are many issues facing Muslims and their freedom to practice their faith overtly or covertly, intertwined with their cultural habits."[15] Some of these issues include inconsistencies in obtaining visas for international speakers, discrimination against Muslim women wearing the hijab, the difficulties in building mosques/schools/community centers, the issues of halal foods and lack of accommodation for prayer, fasting during Ramadan and Islamic dress in the workplace[16].

On an individual level it is critical that equal diligence is given to protecting the religious freedom of a minority faith like Islam. It is important that reactions to Islamophobia do not lead to unwarranted stereotyping and discrimination, as not all Muslims are extremists. However, different principles are required when determining the limitations of religious freedom of the Islamic faith compared to the individual Muslim. Often the laws and social policies that govern the state/federal level on Islamic faith will foster religious freedom as a whole among the general community, but can appear discriminatory and inconsistent to the individual Muslim. This paper will now address the principles that should influence the limitations set for the minority faith of Islam in Australia.

---

[13] Australian Census 2011, http://www.abs.gov.au/ausstats/abs@.nsf/Lookup/2071.0main+features902012-2013 cited May, 2014

[14] *Islam in Australia*, (http://www.immi.gov.au/gateways/police/resources/_pdf/building_bridges.pdf 3 cited May, 2014

[15] Bouma, *Freedom of Religion*, 27-28

[16] Bouma, *Freedom of Religion*, 69

Limitations for Islam in Australia

The great challenge in determining the limits of Islam is first in defining the nature of Islam as a religious entity in Australia. Islam in Australia is culturally and theologically plural by virtue of its diverse social and geographical origins which have brought together Muslims from very different cultural, sectarian, linguistic and national backgrounds[17]. Such diversity can bring confusion when attempting to protect the religious freedom of moderate Islam while setting limits to protect the public interest from the fear of extremist Islam. This paper proposes the following four approaches to Islam when determining its limits as a minority faith at a state/federal level.

Setting Limits on Islam Based on Its Sacred Text and Prophet

Abudallah Saeed highlights a significant point that the perceptions of Islam portrayed in the media and in most available books is far removed from that practised in Australia. It is important to avoid generalisations and stereotypes which become a major obstacle to resolving social and political problems[18]. Such ignorance can lead to fear which in turn potentially lead to violence. He identifies the higher importance of being informed about the religious beliefs and practices of people in one's own country. Islam in Australia is not monolithic in religious expression, but instead pluralistic with varying levels of commitment to Islamic ideas, values and practices[19]. Saeed stresses that Australian Muslims are a group who are loyal and engaged participants in contemporary Australian society.

While Saeed argues a strong case for avoiding stereotypes and generalisations for Australian Muslims, it is difficult to distant

---

[17] The diversity of Muslims can range from the second/third generation hybrids who have a commitment to secular norms at the expense of Islamic/ethnic traditions, to those culturally affiliated with Islam but non practicing to those with a high/low Islam view. A. Saeed & S. Akbarzadeh, *Muslim Communities in Australia,* (Sydney, NSW: UNSW Press 2001), 6 & 35

[18] For example, it is neither accurate nor helpful to suggest that all Muslims believe in a concept of "holy war", such as that expressed by Osama bin Laden and his followers. More broadly, it is not much more helpful to suggest that there are two types of Islam, moderate and extremist, good and bad. Downs, 'Islam in Australia', *Colloquium* 37/1 (2005), 108

[19] Saeed guesses that 30-40% of Australian Muslims are strongly committed while a similar proportion are not; with a range of Muslims being traditionalists, neo-modernists, neo-revivalists and liberals. These categories could be further sub-divided into a range of positions in respect to particular contemporary issues e.g. role of women in family and society. Downs, *Islam in Australia,*108-110

Australian Islam from its global Islamic influence completely. The continual migration of Muslims worldwide, the offshore funding of mosques and educational systems by foreign governments and the recruitment of Imams from outside Australia are doors through which global influence on the religious institutions in the diaspora can still exist[20]. Hence it is prudent that limitations are not set purely on a localized expression of Islam, but set on an Islam defined by the tenets of beliefs and practices stated in the sacred texts (Qur'an and Hadith) and modelled by its ideal model of faith (i.e. Prophet Muhammad).

Another paper reinforces this point through its historical assessment of the cycles of resurgence and decline of Islam. It argues that whenever Islamic power declines the inevitably response to this situation is a resurgence in attention to the Qur'anic roots and to the example of its activist prophet[21]. This is an important distinction as the Qur'an and the example of its prophet comprises beliefs and practices of both peace and violence, resulting in the belief and practice of both a moderate and a radical Islam. Hence whenever there is a reform to the 'true' faith - the Muslim community is held in a tension whether to follow the Muhammad of Mecca (peaceful) or Medina (violent) and unfortunately Islam ends in Medina. While it is wrong to label all Muslims as extremists, it is important to not be ignorant of the issues and set limits on an Islam based on its sacred text and the example of the prophet within which exists the propensity for beliefs and practices that can foster both peace and violence.

Setting Limits on Islam: The Ideology
Islam is more than just a religious creed, it is also political ideology, legal and economic system and social organization[22]. While Christianity has been individualised and privatised under the influence of secular humanism in the West, Islam is a religious force that will not be relegated to the domain of religious isolation nor privatised out of the mainstream of life. For Muslims the whole of life is seamless, interconnected and religious.

---

[20] Funding for mosques is being provided by foreign governments such as Libya, Iran, Iraq, Saudi Arabia, Turkey and the UAE. A. Saeed et al, MCIA, 39-43
[21] *Islam and Europe: Cycles of Resurgence,* (Castle Nuewaldegg, Vienna: Vienna Forum on Post-Christian Europe and Resurgent Islam, 2008), 6
[22] S. Robinson, *Mosques & Miracles - Revealing Islam and God's Grace,* (Upper Mt Gravatt, QLD: City Harvest Publications, 2004), 5

The outworking of Islam as an ideology within a minority faith of 2.2% moderate Muslims, has resulted in widespread impact in every domain of our society in Australia; the establishment of overseas funded mosques[23], certified halal meat[24], charitable and welfare organizations[25], departments and centers of Islamic studies within some of the main educational universities in Australia[26], the quasi-judicial role for Shari'a through the marriage celebrant license[27], attempts at introducing Shari'a Family Law as a parallel system[28] and the establishment of MCCA, the only Islamic financial service provider in Australia[29].

While it can be agreed with Saeed that it is unlikely for Australian Muslims to have a hidden 'single Islamic movement or vision'[30] of a utopian vision of individual morality and government in accordance with Shari'a, nonetheless, the outworking of living Islam's ideology by faithful, moderate Muslims will practically result in Islamisation. This is where equal opportunity does not mean mutual benefit. In protecting their religious freedom as a minority in the name of 'multiculturalism', it is highly possible that the very opportunity can result in the loss of our multiculturalism. Hence it is critical to set limits for Islam as an ideology which means certain limitations may

---

[23] Saeed et al, MCIA, 39

[24] Saeed et al, MCIA, 37

[25] Saeed et. al, MCIA, 38

[26] Centre for Arab and Islamic Studies at Australian National University (http://cais.anu.edu.au); Joint Islamic Studies Program at Monash University and Australian Catholic University, Department of Arabic and Islamic Studies at University of Sydney (http://sydney.edu.au/arts/arabic_islamic/) and National Centre of Excellence for Islamic Studies Australia at Melbourne University (http://nceis.unimelb.edu.au)

[27] Saeed et al, MCIA, 43

[28] In 1989, the Australian Law Reform Commission was asked by the Federal Government to inquire into whether Australian family law was appropriate for a multicultural society. Submissions were made by a number of individual Muslims and Muslim organisations, including the Australian Federation of Islamic Councils, the peak representative body, and the Islamic Council of Victoria. The Commission rejected the proposals raised by the AFIC submission, that different ethnic or religious communities should be able to be governed by their own laws in Australia. Such a decision was received as being insensitive to the needs of religious minorities. Saeed et al, MCIA, 183 & 185

[29] The underlying principle of Islamic finance is that interest is prohibited in the Qur'an and therefore must play no part in the financial and economic activities of a Muslim. This results in different regulations and its performance being unable to be measured against similar operations. MCCA represents the Muslim Community Cooperative of Australia. Saeed et al, MCIA, 188 & 195

[30] Saeed et al, MCIA, 49

be 'discriminatory' or 'inconsistent' when compared to the limitations of other religions.

Some Proposed Limitations:

- There should be equal opportunity for building mosques and churches. However the of sources of external funding of new mosques, their international associations and motivations as well as the teaching content in mosques[31] should be monitored.
- Muslims should be given the freedom to eat halal foods and wear the hijab in public places. However, the autonomy to exercise restrictions should be given to their relevant employers and businesses. Burqas and face coverings should be limited for recognition and safety purposes[32].
- Islamic charities and welfare organizations should be given the same limitations as other religions in the extent to which these platforms can be used to fulfil religio-political purposes.
- Islam should have the same limitations as other religions in the freedom to establish faith studies departments within educational institutions.
- There should be limitations against widespread expansion of Shari'a law as acceptance will result in a parallel legal and finance system that will not benefit our wider society and will run the risk of Islamization through its influence on the domains of our society[33].

Setting Limits on Islam's Use of Other Rights

---

[31] The suspected spiritual leader of Jemaah Islamiah, Abu Bakar Bashir, preached of establishing an Islamic state in Australia in his sermons to Sydney Muslims. In an audio-recording believed to feature his voice, and obtained by the *Sydney Morning Herald*, the hardline cleric gives his broad support to jihad - the term for struggle - to bring Islamic law to the world.
http://www.smh.com.au/articles/2002/12/09/1039379788932.html cited June 2014

[32] This would not be considered discriminatory as it would be applied for anyone of any race and religions.

[33] Islamic law allows a Muslim to use conventional banks, though ordinarily prohibited, in the absence of an Islamic financial situation (*darurah*). However, when a financial situation is established that provides facilities in an Islamically acceptable way, there is an obligation/duty for Muslims to avoid the institutions that engage in Islamically prohibited activities. This implies non Muslim banks as Muslims believe bank interests are prohibited.
It is stated that regarding the profile of MCCA, the organisation should be able to increase its membership particularly as Muslims become increasingly aware of the importance of a commitment to Islam and the need to put into practice Islamic rules and norms, including those related to economic behavior. This implies that if Islamic financial institutions are given widespread acceptance, its influence will change our current economic system. A. Saeed et al, MCIA, 202 & 204

The culture of free speech within the Western world has stirred much controversy among Muslims globally[34]. This has resulted in a 'tone of apology and self-censorship that has settled in many Western policy making arenas'[35]. Muslims have used legislation that outlaws religious vilification but often at the expense of restricting other people's freedom of speech and conscience[36]. The way the laws are being used protects Islam from criticism but silences those who wish to challenge it. This is where tolerance has become less about truth and more about offense[37]. It is important that limits are set on Muslims' use of religious vilification laws as a means of prohibiting other people's freedom to discuss their beliefs with respect to Islam. True religious freedom must empower people to speak their opinions about any religion's doctrines and teachings (including Prophet Muhammad[38]), contentious or otherwise. While such statements may offend Muslims, their 'feelings' are not relevant under the Act.

Setting Limits on Islam: The Majority State
It is critical that limits are set today based on Islam as a majority state. Mission (da'wa) is a fundamental practice of Islam; Islam has become Europe's second largest religion after Christianity within a few decades[39]. Radical clerics such as Abu Bakar Bashir, have urged

---

[34] The Danish cartoon incident, Pope Benedict XVI's speech at Regensberg and Salman Rushdie's *Satanic Verses* has resulted in highly charged Muslim reactions (which included Ayatollah's Khomeini's fatwa declaring Salman an apostate). A. Saeed & H. Saeed, *Freedom of Religion, Apostasy and Islam*, (Burlington, USA: Ashgate Publishing Company, 2004), 1

[35] *Islam and Europe*, 10

[36] In 2002 Pastor Danny Nalliah and Daniel Scot were sued by the Islamic Council of Victoria under Victoria's Racial and Religious Tolerance Act and accused of 'inciting hatred' under religious vilification laws. The case was later dropped.

[37] The Racial and Religious Tolerance Act is supposed to promote religious harmony, but appears to have done the opposite. This is a case where tolerance has shifted from being about truth to offense.

[38] Out of their immense adulation of Muhammad comes an equal anger against any who are said to ridicule the Prophet. J. Melton & M. Baumann, *Religions of the World*, (Denver & Oxford: ABC-CIIO, 2002), 679

[39] Islam gained a permanent religious footing through Muslim migration, consolidation of Muslim identity, the creation of religious and secular institutions to meet the needs of Muslim communities and to act as mediators between them and national/local authorities. The increase in the number of Muslims and the development of such institutions made Islam a visible phenomenon in many European countries – culturally, socially and politically. S. Hunter, *ISLAM, Europe's Second Religion*, (Westport, London: Praegar Publishers, 2002), xiii-xiv

the Islamic faithful in Australia to 'endeavour to bring about an Islamic state in Australia even if it is in 100 years from now'[40]. While Muslims may be a minority, it is important to limit policies today that will enable them to become a majority influence. It is important to limit immigration numbers of Muslims as well as ensuring Shari'a law is not allowed to run parallel to existing social/political structures. While this may appear discriminatory, every sovereign state exercises some form of religious tolerance and limitations. The question that needs to be asked is how religious freedom is practiced in Islamic majority states today[41]? Under an Islamic majority government there is little tolerance, if any, shown to minority groups when compared to the respect minorities receive in our democratic society[42]. To approach Islam as a majority state, while still a minority, is important for determining the trajectory of religious freedom in Australia.

Conclusion

In summary, religious freedom is a fundamental human right. However, there are underlying assumptions that need to be exposed in order to appropriate limitations to religious freedom on minority faiths that will result in welfare of the Australian community. It is important when setting limits to its religious freedom, to not approach Islam as just another religious minority. Instead this paper has proposed four approaches to Islam when setting its limits in religious freedom – Islam defined by its text and prophet, Islam the ideology, Islam and its rights and Islam the majority state.

---

[40] Robinson, *Mosques & Miracles*, 88

[41] When Islam controls, infidels historically have had one of three choices. They may 1) accept Islam after which their lives are spared 2) surrender by a treaty, accepting inferior status and a discriminatory tax 3) be killed by the sword if they are males, or enslaved if women or children. Robinson, *Mosques & Miracles*, 210

[42] "While there is an increase in Muslim minority presence in Western countries, there has been a clamping down on Christian minority activities in Muslim countries, such as Malaysia and Pakistan." *Islam and Europe*, 9

Hindutva

Elizabeth Kendal

Adjunct Research Fellow at the CSIOF
Director of Advocacy
Christian Faith and Freedom.

As evidenced by the Hindu nationalist Bharatiya Janta Party's (BJP's) landslide win in the April-May 2014 polls, India is changing, in more ways than one. Not only did the BJP win 282 of 540 Lok Sabha (federal parliamentary) seats, giving it a simple majority in its own right, but it managed to break out of the Hindu heartland and secure votes from all quarters - geographic and socio-economic.

> *India is changing, in more ways than one.*

When the BJP appointed Gujarat Chief Minister Narendra Modi as its presidential candidate in September 2013, many scoffed, doubting such a controversial, divisive and sectarian figure could lead the BJP to electoral victory. Most analysts believed the Indian electorate would never embrace Modi, especially not the minorities (who are fearful of him) or the educated middle classes (who should know better).

Modi gained notoriety in 2002, when, as Chief Minister of Gujarat, he failed to intervene in Hindu pogroms that left as many as 2000 Muslims dead. Then in 2003, Modi enacted the Gujarat Freedom of Religion Act -- one of India's most draconian anti-conversion laws. In February 2006, Modi oversaw an enormous *Hindutva* campaign in Gujarat's Dang's district, home to the largest concentration of Christians in Gujarat. Hundreds of thousands of Hindus were bussed into Dangs for a non-traditional *kumbh mela* (Hindu pilgrimage) which was supposed to culminate in an anti-Christian pogrom. The vilification and incitement to violence was pervasive, blatant and shocking. Hindutva ideologues popularised the slogan – *"Hindu Jago, Christio Bhagao"* (Arise Hindus, throw out the Christians) – while their cadres ensured all Christian homes were physically identified. Christians believe that the *only* reason a massacre or purge did not ensue was because God intervened "in answer to the prayers of many". (See Religious Liberty Monitoring (RLM): 2006, Jan, Feb, March)

To shift attention away from his image as a sectarian figure, Modi exploited Gujarat's economic development to market himself as India's most successful pro-business administrator – an economic saviour who would raise living standards. Rather than blame the systematic racism of the Hindu caste system for the poverty endemic amongst the minorities, Modi blamed the Congress Party while holding out the "Gujarat model" of economic development as the means by which the BJP would raise living standards for all. Running with the slogan, "*saab ke saath aur saab ka vikas*" (with all, and for everyone's development), Modi was offering the minorities exactly what Congress had failed to deliver: opportunity, as distinct from welfare. [See: RLM post of 2 Oct 2013 – The Modi Operandi of Narendra Modi.]

At a BJP rally in Gujarat on Tuesday 17 Sept 2013, the hugely charismatic Modi managed to persuade some 40,000 Gujarati Muslims to join the party. At a rally in New Delhi on Sunday 29 Sept, the charismatic Modi addressed a crowd of more than 200,000 mostly middle class youths who responded to his lofty promises with "frenzied" excitement. It was, writes political analyst Sanjay Singh, "a public rally, the likes of which it had not seen in many decades". Anil Padmanabhan, another political analyst, remarked (29 Sept 2013) that Modi is connecting with youths and "rapidly becoming a national phenomenon. . . Modi has transcended his party and become a personality".

So what is Hindutva?
Narendra Modi is a self-confessed and proud hinduwadi (supporter of hindutva, i.e. militant Hindu nationalism).

Hindutva is an ideology, which maintains that India -- indeed the entire subcontinent -- is the homeland of the Hindu race. Denying that there ever was an Aryan invasion, Hindutva does not recognise the mostly animist, tribal adivasis (literally: first inhabitants) as the indigenous people of India. Rather, it labels them vanvasis (literally: forest dwellers) and counts them as Hindus, maintaining that the Hindu race is indigenous to India.

Further to this, Hindutva defines a true Hindu as one who acknowledges that India is both his Motherland and his Holy Land. Hindutva maintains that an Indian (a Hindu) who does not recognise India as his holy land cannot be a loyal citizen, for their loyalties are divided.

The missionaries of Hindutva work tirelessly to persuade the traditionally animist adivasis (tribals) that they and the Hindus really are "one people, one nation, one culture" -- i.e. one race. They work to convince the tribals that they are really Hindus whose religion has become corrupted over time. At the same time they Hinduise the adivasis' animistic practices so they don't need to change their practice, just see it as Hindu and self-identify as Hindu.

As for Christians, who belong mostly to scheduled tribes and scheduled castes (also known as Dalits or Untouchables), the Hindutva missionaries tell them that they too were originally Hindus, only their ancestors were either forcibly or fraudulently converted by foreign-invader Christian missionaries.

To motivate the scheduled tribes (8.6 percent) and scheduled castes (16.6 percent) to identify as Hindus, Hindutva holds out the prospect of elevated status; essentially replacing the racial apartheid of caste with religious apartheid -- paving the way for second-class tribals and dalits to become first-class Hindus, superior to any and every non-Hindu.

As a further motivation, and to dragnet the Hindu vote, Hindutva propagates fear, demonising Muslims and Christians as invaders, occupiers and separatists that threaten both social cohesion and national security. Muslims are stereotyped as prolific breeders and terrorists while Christians are accused of being complicit with foreigners in international conspiracies aimed at weakening India through religious conversions. [See: *Preparing the Harvest,* a report by V. K. Shashikumar, Tehelka (magazine), January 2004.]

As a pro-independence revolutionary, V.D. Savarkar (1883-1966) -- regarded as the "Father of Hindutva" -- spent many years in prison during British rule. It was in prison, that Savarkar formulated his Hindutva ideology and wrote what is essentially the handbook on Hindutva. Though he despised the Muslims of the Khilafat movement with whom he was imprisoned, I would suggest that

Savarkar's Hindutva (first edition, 1923) has actually been deeply influenced by Islam.

To fully appreciate the Hindutva view of Christianity, watch the Hindutva documentary: **An Invasion through Conversion** (A video by the Dharma Raksha Samiti, Bangalore (2008) (available on YouTube)

Hindutva has turned India into a tinderbox of communal tension such that today it takes very little to ignite a fire of sectarian hatred that quickly rages out of control.

The goal of *Hindu nationalists* has always been to secure power at the centre and establish India as a Hindu State where the power and privilege of the Hindu elite will be preserved and non-Hindus relegated as second-class citizens to be subjugated, contained and repressed.

The Hindutva family

The umbrella body dedicated to the advancement of Hindutva is known as the **Sangh Parivar**.

The Sangh Parivar comprises the following:

The Rashtriya Swayamsevak Sangh (**RSS**, National Volunteer Corps).

The RSS is a truly massive nation-wide paramilitary force. Founded in Nagpur in 1925 with the mission of creating a Hindu state, the RSS has propagated a militant form of Hinduism as the sole basis for Indian identity. The RSS has access to virtually unlimited funds, as well as a vast network of *swayamsevaks* (volunteers) and *pracharaks* (agitators) who can be mobilised in a moment. Great for politics and persecution.

The founder of the RSS, Madhav Golwalkar, wrote, "foreign race ... must either adopt the Hindu culture and language, must learn to respect and hold in reverence the Hindu religion, must entertain no ideas but those of glorification of the Hindu race and culture ... or may stay in the country wholly subordinated to the Hindu nation, claiming nothing, deserving no privileges, far less any preferential treatment - not even citizen's rights."[1] Nathuram Godse, the assassin who shot and killed Mahatma Gandhi in January 1948, was a member of the RSS. In the dock alongside Godse's was his co-accused: V.D. Savarkar, the "Father of Hindutva". While the foot-soldier Godse was executed, the well-connected Savarkar -- believed to be the brains behind the assassination -- was acquitted on a technicality.

In February 2003, when the Hindu nationalist BJP were in power, they hung a portrait of V.D. Savarkar in the Central Hall of Parliament House, directly opposite the portrait of Mahatma Gandhi.

On 28 May 2014, a day after his inauguration as Prime Minister, Narendra Modi paid tribute to V.D. Savarkar on the 131st anniversary of his birth.

The Vishwa Hindu Parishad (VHP, World Hindu Council) Formed in 1964 to advance Hindutva through cultural means -- i.e. through "saffronised" education, media, conferences and festivals -- the VHP is regarded as the Sangh's "cultural wing". The VHP's work includes missionary endeavours, including the truly massive, high pressure and sometimes violent Ghar Vaspi (literally: homecoming) conversion / "reversion" campaign aimed at bringing Christians "back into the Hindu mainstream".

The Bajrang Dal
The Bajrang Dal is an ultra-violent youth militia. It was formed in 1984 specifically to mobilise Hindu youths for the Ayodhya campaign to seize control of the 16th century Babri Mosque in Ayodhya, Uttar Pradesh, on the spurious grounds that it was the birthplace of the Hindu deity, Ram. On 6 December 1992, rioting Hindus affiliated with the RSS, the VHP and the Bajrang Dal demolished the mosque. The police did not intervene and thousands were killed in the ensuing violence. The controversy is on-going.

The Vanvasi Kalyan Parishad (VKP)

---

[1] Anatomy of India's general election by M K Bhadrakumar, *Asia Times* online, 22 May 2014

The VKP is an offshoot of the RSS comprising militant Hinduised tribals.

The Bharatiya Janta Party (BJP)
The BJP is the political wing of the Sangh Parivar. Founded in December 1980, by 1991 it was India's main opposition party.

1998: In March 1998, the BJP-led National Democratic Alliance (NDA) won the Lok Sabha (federal parliamentary) elections. Running with the slogan, "One People, One Nation, One Culture", and campaigning on a platform that included obtaining nuclear weapons and advancing *Hindutva*. Persecution escalated immediately, and between January 1998 and February 1999, police recorded 116 incidents of violent persecution against Christians -- more than in all the previous 50 years of independence combined. The increased persecution went unremarked (outside Christian media) until Feb 1999, when Bajrang Dal militants ambushed and murdered Australian missionary Graham Staines and his two sons, Philip (10) and Timothy (6), burning them alive in their car in a tribal district of Orissa.

2004: The BJP-led NDA's first term in office was marked by significant economic development, so political analysts across the world were bewildered in 2004 when the BJP was not returned to power. Described in the media as a "shock loss" and "unexplainable", analysts put the BJP's loss down to a widening of the gap between rich and poor that had left multitudes disillusioned. Others maintained that the BJP had diverged from its *Hindutva* path, losing many *Hindutva* supporters in the process (when in reality, the BJP's coalition partners had kept it hamstrung). It must be noted, that the Congress-led United Progressive Alliance (UPA) won the May 2004 Lok Sabha elections by the slimmest of margins.

2009: By mid 2008, disillusionment with the Congress-led UPA government was widespread. In July 2008 the UPA barely survived a no-confidence vote. As 2009 approached, the BJP was favoured to regain power at the centre.

Then, in late November 2008, Islamic militants from Pakistan staged a daring terror attack in Mumbai that left more than 160 dead. While Prime Minister Singh responded with a cool, diplomatic head, negotiating with Pakistan to ensure the killers would be brought to justice, the BJP responded with rhetoric so belligerent that it scared off every swing voter and doubtless many supporters as well. The BJP's election loss in April-May 2009 was *not* a sign that support for *Hindutva* was waning; it was proof that Indians did not want to risk war with Pakistan.

All the while, the VHP's tireless cultural work has met little resistance from secular forces reluctant to tackle *Hindutva* for fear of losing Hindu support. As such, despite the BJP's election losses, despite a decade of Congress-led rule and despite the denials of numerous analysts, *Hindutva* has continued to gain ground. Today *Hindutva's* ascendency can no longer be disputed.

The 2014 election results will have grave consequences for India's more than 71 million Christians (5.8 percent; although many believe the number is closer to 9 percent) whose persecution will now be sanctioned at the highest levels. It will have diabolical consequences for some 83,000 Indian missionaries who now face the prospect of draconian anti-conversion laws being enacted at the national level. I do not believe that this would require a change to the Constitution. It would only require a precedent to establish that the Constitution's religious freedom provisions are to be understood as freedom to hold belief, not freedom to change it; a position that already has wide acceptance, even at the UN.

Elizabeth Kendal is a religious liberty analyst and author of Turn Back the Battle: Isaiah Speaks to Christians Today (Deror Books, Dec 2012). She is an Adjunct Research Fellow at the CSIOF, and the Director of Advocacy at the Canberra-based Christian Faith and Freedom.

elizkendal@crossnet.org.au
9758-5165
2 June 2014

Was Allah testing Zia-ul-Haq? Did he pass the test?

A Pakistan Observer

Throughout his eleven year presidency of Pakistan (1977-88), Islamisation of the nation was one of Zia-ul-Haq's highest priorities. Early in his presidency posters extolling a more fundamentalist type of Islam were readily available from vendors who sat on the side of the road and who displayed them on the nearest wall or pole. One of the posters depicted in one corner a man being whipped, in the other, another having his hand cut off while above these two figures the reading of the Qur'an and the observing of the five prayers was being emphasised. During Ramzan (Ramadan) the fast was strictly enforced, with prosecutions taking place if it was seen being broken. The Zina (Adultery) Ordinance was issued which allowed for women and men who were found guilty to be flogged and if married stoned to death. During Zia-ul-Haq's presidency thousands of women were jailed for adultery or rape because they were not able to produce the 'two male witnesses' needed for their defence. It was during his presidency that the infamous blasphemy laws were introduced. *Nizam-e-Mustafa* - the Islamic system - was the catch cry. Zia ul-Haq's Islamisation was taken further - with implications in economics, the rural sector, education and living.

'What was driving Zia's religious fervour?' Was he just playing into the hands of the many religious political parties that vie for power and authority in Pakistan's politics? Was he playing the religious 'card' in his international diplomacy as he aided the Afghanistan insurgence against the Russian invasion? He certainly allowed the proliferation of madrassa type education in the refugee camps that formed along the border areas between Pakistan and Afghanistan. These camps became a hot bed for fundamentalist Islamic education.

Or was Zia responding to a very personal test? One of Zia's daughters – his oldest daughter though not the oldest child has special needs. What impact did that have on this Muslim family? In a society where honour, with its opposite shame, is deeply imbedded in worldview values, there would have been a sense of shame, possibly deep shame. In most families, a special needs child is hidden away, confined within the walls of the household courtyard. Sadly in that part of the world unless the family is well-educated and has the means of procuring help and assistance, there is virtually no help, assistance or even education as to how to cope with such a situation. Often unseen, the disabled suffer in silence, within the confines of their own homes. Zia's daughter, however, was not so confined. Her family's position, no doubt, gave her opportunities that many other special needs children in that country would never experience. Also by the time Zia was in power, particularly in the capital area of Islamabad/Rawalpindi, where education and medical facilities are more prevalent and modern, there was some recognition of the needs of special needs children. In fact, several centres were established to provide for their needs. Zia's daughter and her mother certainly visited one of them.

For most, the explanation for such a condition is religious. There is an assumption that it's one's fate and so by implication God's will.[1] While at the same time, it might be explained as the result of the power of the evil eye or the outcome of a curse or even the work of an evil spirit. In addition there can also be an underlying innuendo that the mother may have carelessly performed some religious duty or may have even failed to do so.

What was the reason for Zia's daughter's condition? A curse? An evil spirit? The evil eye? Did Zia and/or any members of his family consult with 'holy men' in their attempts to come to terms with the situation? They may well have and the advice would have entailed being more deliberate, more faithful in the practice of religious duties. As an act of God it was their fate; they had to live with it. God was putting them to the test. It was a trial that they just had to face. The typical response is to be more precise and conscientious in one's religious practices, become more 'devout' and to observe the practices with greater zeal. Almost it would seem as a way, albeit in

---

[1] This reference from the Hadith is relevant: "Be sure we shall test you with something of fear and hunger, some loss in goods, lives and the fruits (of your toil) but give glad tidings to those who patiently persevere. Those who, when misfortune strikes them, say: 'Indeed we belong to Allah and to Him is our return. Those are the ones upon whom are blessings and mercy from their Lord and it is those who are rightly guided." [Sûrah al-Baqarah: 155]

some cases subconsciously, of trying to win God's favour to compensate, if it were at all possible, the harsh dealing of the hand of fate, and the seemingly mercilessness of the 'will of Allah'.

So did Zia pass Allah's test? Was he successful in this trial? What legacy did Zia leave in Pakistan? Certainly in the religious arena, Islamic fundamentalism vies uneasily with more moderate and liberal ideas. Much of the country is seething with unrest – not always religiously based, though skilfully used by the religious parties and groups to increase the discontent. The Ahmadiyya minority within the country has virtually become stateless; the Christian minority all too well knows the force of the blasphemy laws and feels the terror associated with burnings and bomb blasts. Legally the system is in confusion with a constant emphasis on introducing Islamic laws. While, at the same time the more liberal system inherited from the British is being pitted against Islamic Shari'a law. Generally the more powerful side uses the particular legal system that will achieve the results it wants irrespective of the legality of their claim. Though there has been some legislation passed to bring the madrassas into line with general education, the influence of the fundamentalist Islamic schools of the refugee camps has found its way into the warp and woof of both rural and urban society. That teaching is being played out in bomb blasts and terrorist acts that resound throughout the country with the call to make Pakistan more Islamic.

Ahmadis:
A Minority in the Context of Pakistan

Qaiser Julius
PhD Researcher

Melbourne School of Theology

Introduction
In Pakistan, it isn't just the Christians who suffer persecution. This article explores the nature of oppression for the Ahmadis, another religious minority in Pakistan.

A brief history of the Ahmadiyya Movement
The Ahmadiyya movement was founded in 1889, during the British Raj, by Mirza Ghulam Ahmad at Qadian, a small town located in Punjab, India. Ghulam Ahmad was born there in 1835, and learned both Persian and Arabic through home tutoring. Ahmad's biographers say that he showed a great interest in religious literature from his early youth.[1] As a young man in Sialkot (1864-68), Ghulam Ahmad had religious debates with Christian missionaries.[2] Some commentators suggest that, due to his encounters with Christians, "some initial organizational ideas took shape in his mind for the cause of Islam."[3] A turning point in his life came in 1889, when he claimed, through a divine revelation, the right to accept *baya* (allegiance given to a religious leader).[4] Moreover, two

---

[1] F.K. Khan Durrani, (1927), *The Ahmadiyya Movement*, Lahore: The Ahmadiyya Anjuman-i-Ishaat-i-Islam, 22.

[2] A. R. Dard, (2008) *Life of Ahmad: Founder of the Ahmadiyya Movement,* Tilford, Surrey: Islam International Publications, 48-49.

[3] Spencer Lavan, (1974) *The Ahmadiyyat Movement: A History and Perspective*, Delhi: Manohar Book Service, 31; H. A. Walter, (1918) *The Ahmadiya Movement,* Calcutta: Association Press, 14.

[4] First covenant ceremony took place at Ludhiana in 1889 where forty followers showed allegiance to him. See Mirza Bashir-ud-Din Mahmud Ahmad, Hadhrat Ahmad, (1998), Ohio: Islam International Publications, http://www.alislam.org. 27. (Editor's note: 'baya' is regarded as form of divine authorisation to perform religious roles and have religious authority. In some cases it can involve an elaborate ceremony.)

years later in 1891, Ahmad claimed to be the promised Messiah expected by Christians and Jews as well as the *Imam Mehdi* expected by Muslims.[5] These claims made him a highly controversial figure which is evident from the fact that, before he died in May 1908, he was denounced as an imposter and his followers were labelled *kafir* (infidel), *taghut* (devil), *murtadd* (apostate) and *munafiq* (hypocrite) by orthodox Islamic authorities.[6] This study of Ahmadis' experience in Pakistan is divided into four chronological periods.

The First Wave of the Anti-Ahmadi Campaign (1947-1950)
When Pakistan came into existence in 1947, the anti-Pakistan leaders of Islamic parties found no place for their politics in India, so, despite their opposition to the new nation, they were compelled to migrate to Pakistan. They brought with them their legacy, "the curse of *Takfir* (calling one another infidel)... and their first target was the Ahmadis."[7] The seed of the Ahmadi controversy in Pakistan was sown by the Majilis-i-Ahrar-i-Islam (Committee for the Freedom of Islam) which was a religio-political party. On arrival in Pakistan, the Ahrar changed its name from "Majilis-i-Ahrar-i-Islam-i-Hind" to "All Pakistan Majilis-i-Ahrar."[8] After the Ahrar had acquired a new identity, they started to campaign against the Ahmadis in their new homeland: "On May 1, 1949, Ahrar activists made their first public demand that Ahmadis be declared a non-Muslim minority."[9] In response to Ahrar's anti-Ahmadi call, a young military officer, Major Mahmud, was stoned and stabbed to death by a violent mob in Quetta.[10] The central government of Pakistan took stern action against the Ahrar, and a number of their leaders were arrested and tried in court. Thus, the Ahrar's initial move against the Ahmadis was discouraged by the newly established government of Pakistan.

---

[5] Mirza Ghulam Ahmad, (2002) *Fateh Islam* [Victory of Islam, Tilford, Surrey: Islam International Publications,).

[6] Naveeda Khan, (2012) *Muslim Becoming: Aspiration and Skepticism in Pakistan* Durham: Duke University Press, 109.

[7] Muhammad Munir, (1980) *From Jinnah to Zia*, 2nd ed.,Lahore: Vanguard Books, 38.

[8] Surendra Nath Kaushik, (1996) *Ahmadiya Community in Pakistan: Discrimination, Travail, and Alienation*, South Asia Studies Series, New Delhi: South Asian Publishers, 24.

[9] Mansoor Ahmed Shah, (2008), "1974: Anit-Ahmadi Hostilities," *The Review of Religions* 103, no. 3: 54.

[10] M. Munir and M.R. Kayani, 1954), *Report of the Court of Inquiry Constituted under Punjab Act II of 1954 to enquire into the Punjab disturbances of 1953*, Lahore: Government of Punjab, 13-14.

The Second Wave of the Anti-Ahmadi Campaign (1950-53)
However, after a brief pause, the Ahrar reactivated their campaign against the Ahmadis in 1950. The Ahrar reproduced a pamphlet called *Ash-Shahab*, which contained a *fatwa* that Ahmadis were *murtadds* (apostates). Under Islamic law, the penalty for apostasy is death.[11] The pamphlet was widely circulated in Punjab and frequently cited by Ahrar's leaders in their public speeches during the 1950s. Their speeches provoked a new wave of sectarian violence against the Ahmadis in the Punjab region resulting in killings, looting and burning the worship places of Ahmadis.[12]

Finally, an ultimatum was given to the government that "if within a month the Ahmadis were not declared a non-Muslim minority... [Action Committee] would resort to direct action."[13] In response, the government rejected their demands and arrested some of their key leaders. This Government action mostly affected the Punjab, where several Ahmadis were killed and their mosques and property burnt and looted.[14] The violence increased to such a level that the government imposed martial law in the Punjab in order to restore law and order.

The Third Wave of the Anti-Ahmadi Campaign (1973-74)
After twenty years, the anti-Ahmadiyya movement was again launched in February 1974. Pressure mounted to change the legal status of Ahmadis. This demand exerted tremendous pressure on Zulfikar Ali Bhutto, then the Prime Minister, who brought the issue forward to the parliament of Pakistan. Subsequently, a Constitutional Amendment was unanimously passed by the Parliament on 7th September 1974, in which Ahmadis were declared non-Muslims.[15] It was unprecedented that "for the first time the parliament passed judgment on the beliefs of a community and declared it non-Muslims".[16] Some considered that the state had

---

[11] Ibid., 18; Kaushik, *Ahmadiya Community in Pakistan*: 26.

[12] Kayani, *Report of the Court of Inquiry*: 30.

[13] Ibid., 1.

[14] Munir, *From Jinnah to Zia*: 38.

[15] *Act 49 of 1974: Constitution (Second Amendment) Act*, (September 17, 1974) 26 P.L.D Central Statutes (1974), 425.

[16] Shaikh Aziz, (2013) "A Leaf from History: The Ahmadi Issue," *Dawn*, 24 February http://dawn.com.

gone far beyond its mandate because the matter of someone's belief is a personal issue between him and God and should not be the business of the state:[17] As Jinnah, founder of Pakistan, had clearly said, "you belong to any religion or caste or creed that has nothing to do with the business of the State."[18]

The Fourth Wave of the Anti-Ahmadi Campaign (1980-84)

During General Zia-ul-Haq's dictatorial rule (1977 – 1988) persecution of Ahmadis intensified due to the resurgence of orthodox Islam. In 1980, Zia imposed mandatory Islamic taxes: *zakat* (wealth tax) and *ushr* (agricultural tax), on Muslims.[19] Although the Shia Muslims opposed it vehemently[20] *Jammat-i-Ahmadiya* declared on 28 July 1980 that "Ahmadiyas are Muslims and they will continue to pay *zakat* and *ushr*..."[21] However, this statement refuelled anti-Ahmadi sentiments in Orthodox circles. Consequently anti-Ahmadi forces reorganized themselves under the umbrella of *Tehrik-i-Tahfuz-i-Khatm-i-Nabuwat* (Movement for the Protection of the Last Prophet (hood) - TKN). They demanded that Zia-ul-Haq resolve the confusion which still existed regarding the status of Ahmadis in Pakistan, even though they had been constitutionally declared non-Muslims in 1974.[22] Zia met the demand of the anti-Ahmadis on 8th April 1981 by passing the Provisional Constitutional Order, which, in sections 1-A (a) and (b), defined Muslims and non-Muslims.[23] Again, on 12 April 1982,

> " ... *you belong to any religion or caste or creed that has nothing to do with the business of the State.*"
> M A Jinnah,
> Founder of Pakistan

---

[17] Yasser Latif Hamdani, (2012) "The 1974 National Assembly Proceedings on the Ahmadi Issue," *Daily Times*, 22 October, http://dailytimes.com.pk.

[18] Mahomed Ali Jinnah, (1962) *Quaid-i-Azam Mahomed Ali Jinnah: Speeches as Governor-General of Pakistan 1947-48*, Karachi: Pakistan Publications, 9.

[19] *Ordinance 28 of 1980: Zakat and Ushr Ordinance*, (June 20, 1980) 32 P.L.D Central Statutes (1980), 97. This ordinance authorized the government to deduct 2.5% from bank deposits and to levy one tenth (1/10) on gross proceeds of land possessed by the Muslims.

[20] Shia tradition believes in the voluntary *zakat*.

[21] Kaushik, *Ahmadiya Community in Pakistan*: 60.

[22] Ibid.

[23] " 'Muslim' means a person who believes...in the absolute and unqualified finality of the Prophethood of Muhammad (PBUH)... and 'non-Muslim' means a person who is not a Muslim and includes a person belonging to the Christian, Hindu,... a person of Quadiani group or the Lahori group (who call themselves Ahmadis or by any other name)..." *C.M.L.A*

Zia clarified the State's position through a presidential order which reaffirmed that Ahmadis are non-Muslims.[24]

Nevertheless, none of these measures satisfied the demands of the TKN. They put pressure on Zia, renewing their demands for "immediate implementation of the Islamic punishment for apostasy which is not less than [the] death sentence; [a] complete ban on the publication and distribution of Ahmadiya literature..."[25] Zia acceded to their demands, but in a slightly different way. He issued Ordinance 20 in 1984, which added two new sections, 298-B and C to the Pakistan Penal Code (PPC). [26] This Ordinance prohibited Ahmadis from calling their *Azan* (Prayer-call), preaching and propagating their faith, calling their faith Islam, or presenting themselves as Muslim. [27]

Ordinance 20 caused great concern to Ahmadis and they immediately approached the Federal Shari'at Court (FSC), asking it to exercise its mandate under Article 203-D[28] of the Constitution of Pakistan to examine whether or not Ordinance 20 was in conflict with the injunctions of the Qur'an and Sunnah.[29] However, the FSC upheld the validity of Ordinance 20 and dismissed the petition. [30]

After losing their battle in the FSC, a large number of Ahmadis were prosecuted and convicted in the different courts of the country. The Ahmadis were left with no choice but to take their case to the Supreme Court of Pakistan (SCP) claiming that Ordinance 20

Order 2 of 1981: Provisional Constitution (Amendment) Order, (April 07, 1981) 33 P.L.D Central Statutes (1981), 310-11.

[24] *President's Order 8 of 1982: Amendment of the Constitution (Declaration) Order*, (April 12, 1982) 34 P.L.D Central Statutes (1982), 164-65.

[25] Kaushik, *Ahmadiya Community in Pakistan*: 63.

[26] *Ordinance 20 of 1984: Anti-Islamic Activities of Quadiani Group, Lahori Group and Ahmadis (Prohibition and Punishment) Ordinance*, (April 26, 1984) 36 P.L.D Central Statutes (1984), 102-03.

[27] Ibid.

[28] President's Order 1 of 1980: Constitution (Am*endment) Order,* (May 26, 1980) 32 P.L.D Central Statutes (1980). Article 203-D states: "If any law or provision of law is held by the Court to be repugnant to the Injunctions of Islam and such law or provision shall, to the extent to which it is held to be so repugnant, cease to have effect on the day on which the decision of the Court takes effect." See also *President's Order 5 of 1982: Constitution (Second Amendment) Order*, (March 22, 1982) 34 P.L.D Central Statutes (1982), 155-56.

[29] *Majibur Rehman and 3 Others v. Federal Government of Pakistan*, 37 P.L.D 8, 17 (1985).

[30] Ibid.

violates the fundamental rights guaranteed under Article 20 of the Constitution of Pakistan.[31] One of the legal counsels of the Ahmadiyya community, Majib-ur-Rehman, argued that Article 20 "cannot be suspended even under emergency declared under Article 232 of the Constitution."[32] Despite their best efforts, on 3rd July 1993, the SCP dismissed all eight appeals on two grounds: firstly, the religious practice of Ahmadis offends the majority of Muslims in Pakistan; and secondly, the Islamic use of epithets by Ahmadis violates the company and trademark laws.[33]

With this judgment by the top judiciary of the country, all the legal doors for the Ahmadis have been completely shut in Pakistan. Since then, the situation for the Ahmadiyya community has rapidly deteriorated: as Hoodbhoy, a renowned Pakistani scholar, noted, "Ahmadis are the lightning rod that attracts more hatred than any other sect."[34]

> *With this judgment by the top judiciary of the country, all the legal doors for the Ahmadis have been completely shut in Pakistan.*

It is pertinent to note since 1984 it has become increasingly difficult for the Ahmadiyya community in Pakistan. Since then, hate-filled posters, stickers, fliers and calendars have been openly distributed, inciting people to kill Ahmadis.[35] For example, pamphlets were distributed in Faisalabad in 2011 "audaciously displaying names and addresses of 50 prominent Ahmadis who were to be eliminated."[36] Even the government offices in Lahore display a poster containing hate speech against Ahmadis. One of the posters at the Lahore's Custom House reads: "*Jo Qadiani ka yar hai ghaddar*

---

[31] Article.20 (a) "Every citizen shall have the right to profess, practice and propagate his religion; and
b) Every religious denomination and every sect thereof shall have the right to establish, maintain and manage its religious institutions."

[32] Mujeeb-ur-Rehman, (2002), Error at the Apex, Ontario, Canada Oriental Publishers, http://www.thepersecution.org.

[33] *Zaheer-ud-din v. The State*, (1995) S.C.M.R 1718(1993). For good analysis of Supreme Court's ruling see Nadeem Ahmad Saddiq, "Enforced Apostasy: Zaheeruddin v. State and the Official Persecution of the Ahmadiyya Community in Pakistan," *Law and Inequility* 14 (1995).

[34] Zofeen T. Ebrahim,(2011), "Ahmadis: The Lightning Rod that Attracts the Most Hatred," *Dawn*, October 28, http://dawn.com.

[35] Staff Reporter, (2012) "Hate Compaign against Ahmadis Reaches New Height " *Daily Times*, May 05, 16.

[36] Editor, (2012) "A Community No One Cares About," *The Express Tribune*, June 18, 06.

ghaddar hai (whoever is a friend of an Ahmadi is a traitor)".[37] Another poster in front of the banking court in Lahore reads: "When a Muslim befriends a Qadiani he causes anguish to the Holy Prophet."[38] From this, it can be deduced that the government was frightened by the religious forces.[39]

As a result of the hate posters, many Ahmadis were killed in several parts of Pakistan. The campaign against Ahmadis reached a zenith on 28 May 2010, when two Ahmadi worship places in Lahore were stormed by religiously motivated attackers with modern weapons, who killed 95 Ahmadi worshippers and severely injured over 120.[40] The Ahmadiyya community expressed their feelings in a letter to the President and Prime Minister of Pakistan, saying that "we have been left by the state at the mercy of the militants and miscreants who are thirsty for Ahmadi blood."[41] Moreover Ahmadis are single out for special vilification. When acquiring a Pakistani Passport a Muslim must declare: "I consider Mirza Ghulam Ahmad Qadiani to be an imposter *nabi* [prophet] and also consider his followers…to be NON-MUSLIMS."[42] (emphasis mine)

Conclusion
This article has demonstrated that Ahmadis have been facing religious, legal, social and political discrimination which makes them one of the most vulnerable minority groups in Pakistan. Because of this, many of them seek asylum in Europe, the USA or Australia. Ahmadis have been facing severe hostility from orthodox Muslims who consider them not only heretics but also *kafir*, so deserving of death. The Ahmadiyya community migrated to Pakistan in 1947 in anticipation of a better life in a Muslim country, because they identify themselves as Muslims but it proved completely the opposite. This discussion leads us to conclude that the more religious or Islamic Pakistan has become, the more sectarian it has become.

---

[37] Yasser Latif Hamadani, (2012) "Do Ahmadis Deserve to Live in Pakistan?," *The Friday Times*, August 08.
[38] Ibid.
[39] Zaeem Qadri, (2010), Advisor to the Chief Minister of Punjab, Interview on Dunya TV on 30 May
[40] Salman Aslam, (2010) "Ahmadis Worship Places Hit; 80 Killed," *Dawn*, May 29, 01; Faisal Ali,(2010) "95 Killed in Lahore Claim Ahmadis," *Dawn*, May 30, 01.
[41] Saba Imtiaz, (2012) "As death toll mounts Ahmadis fight back with letters," *The Express Tribune*, November 02, 02.
[42] Pakistani Passport Application Form, available at http://www.dgip.gov.pk

Honour Crimes
The concept of honour within Islam, Honour-based violence and a Christian Response

Amelia Gibson*
Graduate Student

Melbourne School of Theology

Honour Crimes
Honour is a key facet to many world religions. Their texts and instructions provide their believers information on how to be honourable or maintain honour within society. The concept of maintaining 'family honour' is especially paramount to the religion and practice of Islam. In Islam honour-based violence, predominantly perpetrated by family members, is a practice that has been prevalent for centuries. Whilst honour crimes do not only occur in Islamic societies, research indicates that the overwhelming majority of honour killings do happen amongst Muslim communities in the East and West with young women as the victims.[1] When social status, tradition and modern society interlocks, even more so with the increasing globalisation of the 21st century, cultural and religious expectations are challenged, resulting in many Muslims societies, in fear and inevitably violence. How can Christians respond to this emerging issue? The following essay will focus on the idea of honour in Islam and the Qur'an, the motivations behind honour based violence focussing on a number of cases and a Christian biblical response to this horrific issue.

Honour Killings: A Definition
'Honour killing' is defined as 'maintaining of family honour through the murder of a family member accused of violating the honour of

---

*Amelia Gibson is a pseudonym
[1] Phyllis Chesler, (2010), 'Worldwide Trends in Honor Killings' in *Middle East Quarterly* (Spring); http://www.meforum.org/2646/worldwide-trends-in-honor-killings cited 2 August, 2014

their family'.[2] An example of this violation is when a woman is accused of having a forbidden relationship with a member of the opposite sex,[3] when a couple marry against the wishes of their family or when a wife seeks divorce from her husband, tainting the honour of her family.[4] There are also multiple instances whereby women are killed for having reported rape; thirteen year old Aisha Ibrahim Duhulow was publicly stoned to death by the Al-Shabab militia in Kismayo, Somalia in 2008 for a punishment for bringing shame on Islam.[5]

The United Nations estimate that 5000 women are killed each year in the name of honour; however, it is widely acknowledged that this number is likely to be much higher; many women simply go missing.[6] Countries known for their practice of honour based violence include Bangladesh, India, Pakistan, Egypt, Iraq and Jordan, Turkey and in Muslim communities in the UK and the USA.[7] Reports overwhelmingly indicate that the practice of honour killings targets young women (the average age for a victim of an honour crime is 23 years old)[8] and is an act of protecting the social, cultural and religious norms of the society in which the family lives.

The Concept of Honour in Honour/Shame Cultures

Honour killings are most prevalent in cultures where the concepts of honour and shame are at the core of social standing. Although not exclusively, this honour shame culture, along with honour-based violence, can be seen most clearly amongst cultural Muslim communities in both the East and the

> *Honour killings are most prevalent in cultures where the concepts of honour and shame are at the core of social standing.*

---

[2] Sally Ekkary, et al, (2014), 'Honour crimes: review and proposed definition' in *Forensic Science, Medicine and Pathology 10/1* (March), 76

[3] Joanna Bond, (2012), 'Honor as Property', *Columbia Journal of Gender and Law* 23/2 203

[4] Bond, 'Honor as Property', 203

[5] Amnesty International, 'Child of 13 stoned to death in Somalia', *Amnesty* http://www.amnesty.org/en/news-and-updates/news/child-of%20-13-stoned-to-death-in-somalia-20081031 (31st October 2008) cited 29 May, 2014

[6] Mohammad M Idriss & Tahir Abbas, (2011). *Honour, Violence, Women and Islam* (Oxon: Routledge,

[7] Gill Hague, Aisha K. Gill, and Nazand Begikhani (2013), "Honour'-based violence and Kurdish communities: moving towards action and change in Iraqi Kurdistan and the UK' in *Journal of Gender Studies* 22/4 (December), 386

[8] Chesler, 'Worldwide Trends in Honour Killings', 3

West. In a study carried out analysing 230 honour killing incidents, ninety one percent were found to be Muslim.[9] The two main motives identified in these cases were being 'too Western' and 'sexual impropriety'.[10] Giordano describes how in honour-shame cultures, a competition for honour, reputation and status is created, generating fear of social shaming, leading to justification of honour based violence.[11] Furthermore, Zvinkliene discusses how the deeper patriarchy is embedded into a culture, and with honour shame cultures this is often the case, the more the control of women and stricter expectation that they must conform to social systems.[12] Male relatives who carry out these honour killings are often seen as 'heroic' and show little remorse; we will discuss this later with in depth case studies.

The concept of 'honour as property' has also been explored by author and Law Professor Johanna Bond, who examines the idea of honour as a 'social currency' and how the value of honour is placed on a woman conforming her behaviour, sexual or otherwise, to the expectations of her family and society around her.[13]

> *In societies where honour based violence occurs, women's behaviour and body are seen as being entirely controlled and therefore 'owned' by men.*

In societies where honour based violence occurs, women's behaviour and body are seen as being entirely controlled and therefore 'owned' by men[14] especially the woman's husband, father or brothers. Bond states that within these communities, 'although women are not typically seen as holders of honour property, women play a significant role in determining its value to the family as a whole'.[15] This then allows the male members of the family to 'take back' this honour through violence. There is much debate as to whether it is religion or culture which

---

[9] Chesler, 'Worldwide Trends in Honour Killings', 1

[10] Chesler, 'Worldwide Trends in Honour Killings', 1

[11] Giordano, Christian. (2010) 'Honour in different cultures and legal systems,' *Islam and Civilisation Renewal* 1/4, 687

[12] Zvinkliene, Alina, (2010), 'Honour Killings in Modern Societies: A Sociological Perspective', *Islam and Civilisation Renewal* 1/3 535

[13] Bond, 'Honour as Property', 206

[14] Bond, 'Honour as Property', 206

[15] Bond, 'Honour as Property', 205

fuels honour-based violence and how the treatment of women influences statistics.[16] Let's examine some key Qur'anic texts on this issue.

Islam, Women and Honour-based Violence
Before we examine honour-based violence in itself we must look at the cultural and religious teaching regarding women, who make up the majority of victims, in the societies in which this violence occurs. There are varying degrees of contradictions and conflicting information given within Islamic teaching about the treatment of women. Whilst the Islamic prophet, Muhammad, spoke out against female infanticide, cruel treatment of women and female prostitution, he himself had multiple wives, his youngest of which was 6 years old (he consummated the marriage at age 9) and many concubines.[17] The Qur'an, (2:282) implies the inferiority of women and their intellect, giving permission to beat them if they rebel. (In Q 4:34, the Arabic word used is *idribuhunna*, meaning with 'light force'). In the Hadith, women are described as evil and the inhabitants of hell, equal to dogs and donkeys. Unlike men they are not permitted to marry outside the religion of Islam (Q 5:6). As women are to be under the control of men women seen as tainting family honour may be killed since the shedding of blood is seen as restoring honour.

The Qur'an teaches that men are managers of the affairs of women because Allah has made the one superior to the other (Q4:34)[18] and that wives are a *tilth*, or field, for men to use at will (Q 2:223). Many have used Sura 4:15 in carrying out honour-based violence. This states that women who are found guilty of committing unlawful sexual intercourse (four male witnesses need to verify this according to Sura 2:282 because of the

> *The Qur'an teaches that men are managers of the affairs of women because Allah has made the one superior to the other (Q4:34)1 and that wives are a tilth, or field, for men to use at will (Q 2:223).*

---

[16] Zvinkliene, 'Honour Killings'.536

[17] References to this marriage are recorded in the Hadith: Sahih al-Bukhari, 5:58:234, 5:58:236, 7:62:64, 7:62:65, 7:62:88, Sahih Muslim, 8:3309, 8:3310, 8:3311, 41:4915, Sunan Abu Dawood, 41:4917

[18] Anonymous, (2009), 'The Challenge to Biblical Christians of the Islamic Theology of Women,' *Priscilla Papers* 23/1), 16

"deficiency of women's minds") must be confined until death or Allah takes her.[19]

Adultery is punishable by one hundred public lashings (Q 24:2) and stoning to death (Muslim 17:4209, al-Bukhari 6:60:79). Al-Bukhari (7:63:196) tells the story of the Prophet Muhammad ordering the stoning to death of a man who had committed adultery. Sahih Muslim (01:4206) tells the story of a woman who became pregnant, outside of marriage, and presented herself to the Prophet Muhammad for punishment. She was ordered to be buried to the neck and stoned. Whilst Islamic texts speak of equal punishment for the man and woman involved, evidence suggest that women are much more likely to be killed for such behaviour. In a number of Islamic communities, men who commit honour based violence (mainly husbands, fathers or brothers) are penalised lightly by law or simply ignored by officials, claiming it a 'domestic' affair and justified under Shari'a law[20]; this includes countries such as Jordan where their Penal Code outlines the person responsible for murder of an adulteress should be exempt.

Those who speak for Islam in the public sphere including Islamic authors, lecturers and religious leaders give differing opinions on the justification of honour-based violence in the Islamic texts. Many of them deny any parallel between the Islamic texts and honour killing. A number of research reports published by 'Islam Awareness' and various PhD papers highlight that the Qur'an has an inherently high value on human life and does not permit the murder of any other (Q5:32).[21] Muslim scholar Sheikh Muhammad Al-Hanooti, member of the North American Fiqh Council stated that there is no place in Islam for unjustifiable killing arguing that even capital punishment can only be carried out by the government.[22] On the other hand, whilst Tahira Shahid Khan, a professor on women's issues at the Aga Khan University in

---

[19] 'Islam and Women' in *Answering Islam.com* http://www.answering-islam.org cited on 29th May, 2014

[20] Anonymous, *The Challenge to Biblical Christians of the Islamic Theology of Women*, 16

[21] Islam Awareness, 'Honour Killings.' http://www.islamawareness.net/HonourKilling/dissertation_is_and_hon_crimes.pdf cited 21st July 2014

[22] Islam Awareness, 'Dissertation: Islam and Honor Crimes,' http://www.islamawareness.net/HonourKilling/dissertation_is_and_hon_crimes.pdf, (cited on 2nd August 2014), 40 cited 21st July, 2014

Pakistan, states that she believes the Qur'an does not justify honour killing, Islamic culture promotes 'the concept of ownership [which] has turned women into a commodity which can be exchanged, bought and sold.'[23] This idea of women as property owned by men creates an environment where women are used by men as the maintainers of honour and therefore also the cleansing of shame. Reporter and foreign correspondent for the *Gaza Gajeera*, Al Skudsi bin Hookah describes his view of Islam and honour killings in the following statement:

> '*Deep down, we know that when a woman has disgraced her family, nothing will restore honor except by killing her. This is understood in Jordan, Syria, Yemen, Lebanon, Egypt, the Gaza strip and the West Bank. So why are we Arabs telling the Western press that honor killing is cultural, that it is not really part of Islam? Our way of life is based on maintaining our honor. And make no mistake about it: a woman does tarnish her family's honor by engaging in pre-marital sex, or by getting herself raped, when she seeks divorce and when she marries against her family's wishes. And keeping our women pure is a big part of our honor. So there's no point saying honor killing isn't really part of our religion. Honor and Islam are inextricably bound; they are what give our life meaning. A strong religion demands we choose to maintain our honor.*'[24]

With these varied views on honour-based violence within Islam, how does Islamic opinion and Islamic teaching play out in Islamic government worldwide?

Honour Based Violence in Pakistan and Iraq
The Human Rights Commission of Pakistan reported that nine hundred reports of honour crimes had occurred in 2013 in the country alone but suspected that many more had occurred without the knowledge of the HRC.[25] A study within the District Shikarpur, Sindh, Pakistan found that women were very rarely given the

---

[23] Hillary Mayall, 'Thousands of Women Killed for Family "Honor"', http://news.nationalgeographic.com.au/news/2002/02/0212_020212_honorkilling_2.html cited 21st July 2014.
[24] Syed Kamran Mirza, 'Honour Killing is Absolutely Islamic', http://www.islam-watch.org/syedkamranmirza/honor_killing.htm (cited 2nd August 2014).
[25] Anwar Syed, et al, *Domestic Violence Against Women: A Case Study of Shikarpur, Sindh Pakistan*, 116.

opportunity to defend themselves and those accused of violating their family or communities' honour were considered shameful even after their death; their bodies often thrown into rivers and buried in mass graves.[26] The term 'kari' (tr. blackened woman) is given to women who are accused of defiling the family honour; they are subject to rape, torture and often death usually at the hands of close male relatives.[27] The recent honour killing of pregnant Pakistani woman, Farzana Parveen, made world headlines. Mrs Parveen was stoned to death outside a Pakistani court by twenty male family members, her father being the main instigator, on Tuesday 27th May 2014[28] for marrying a man without her families' permission. Mrs. Parveen's father accused his daughter of dishonouring the family; "I killed my daughter as she had insulted all of our family by marrying a man without our consent, and I have no regret over it."[29] Did Q24:2 have an influence in this father's decision or is it purely cultural?

Amidst the Kurdish community of Northern Iraq, reports have indicated that honour-based violence is increasing with the clash of the traditional tribal and Islamic laws and the rapid modernisation of the countries' north.[30] In Kurdistan, the result of dishonouring (tr. a'r) codes of social conduct (as outlined by family), whether this be by going out without permission or having forbidden contact with a man, could be coercion, genital mutilation, forced abortion and rape. Kurdish Sirwa Hama Amin married a man her family disapproved of and as such, four months after their marriage, her brother hunted down and killed her husband and attempted to kill her in an honour-based violent attack in 2010.[31] A Jordanian man was imprisoned for six months after killing his sister who had been raped, exclaiming, and "I would rather die than lose my honour ...

---

[26] Anwar Syed, et al, 116.

[27] Anwar Syed et al, 117

[28] Heather Saul, 'Lahore 'Honour Killing': Farzana Parveen was pregnant when she was stoned to death for marrying man she loved' in *Independent UK* (May 28 2014). http://www.independent.co.uk/news/world/asia/lahore-honour-killing-farzana-iqbal-was-pregnant-when-she-was-stoned-to-death-for-marrying-man-she-loved-9444887.html cited 29 May, 2014

[29] Heather Saul, 'Lahore 'Honour Killing': Farzana Parveen was pregnant when she was stoned to death for marrying man she loved' in *Independent UK* (May 28 2014).

[30] Hague et al, Honour-based Violence and Kurdish Communities: Moving Towards Action and Change in Iraqi Kurdistan and the UK, 386

[31] John Leland and Namo Abdulla, , 'A Killing Set Honor Above Love' in *The New York Times* (November 20th 2010) http://www.nytimes.com/2010/11/21/world/middleeast/21honor.html?pagewanted&_r=0

Our whole life is founded on honour. If we lose it, we have no life, we become swine ... We're no better than animals."[32]

Honour-based Violence in the West

Honour crimes have also become an increasing concern for the West as well. The UK Metropolitan Police, in 2009, recorded a significant rise in the reports of honour-based violence.[33] A Kurdish woman, Banaz Mahmood, who was living in the UK, was strangled by her father and uncle for leaving her arranged marriage to be with another man.[34] Afghani born Mohammad Shafia was convicted of murdering his first wife and three daughters in Canada in 2009 because he stated he was becoming increasingly unhappy with their 'secret boyfriends and revealing clothing'.[35] These are just two of many highly publicised cases.

A Biblical Response

How do Christians respond to this concept of defending 'family honour' through violence? Especially as honour based violence is primarily a gendered violence, what does the Bible have to say about the treatment and role of women? In Old Testament cultures, honour was virtually if not of equal importance to what it is to Islamic cultures today. The Law of Moses outlines the strict instructions by which the Israelites are to live, including social, food and purity laws. However with the example of Jesus, the concept of honour and the perception and treatment of women is re-shaped. In John 7:53-8:11, the religious rulers brought a woman to Jesus who has been caught in adultery for judgement. In contrast to the Qur'anic (and Mosaic Law for that matter) where adulterers are to be stoned to death, Jesus instead says 'let anyone among you who is without sin be the first to throw a stone at her.' Jesus consistently showed compassion towards women throughout the gospels (Mark 7:24-30, Matt 8:14-15); including healing women who were considered 'unclean' (Mark 5:25-34) or 'unholy' (Mark 5:35-43). He

---

[32] Bond, 'Honour as Property', 207

[33] 'Banaz Mahmod 'honour' Killing Cousins Jailed for Life' in BBC *News* UK (10th November, 2010) http://www.bbc.com/news/uk-england-london-11716272 cited 29 May, 2014

[34] 'Banaz Mahmod 'Honour' Killing Cousins Jailed for Life' in BBC *News* UK (10th November, 2010) http://www.bbc.com/news/uk-england-london-11716272 cited 29 May, 2014

[35] Martin Patriquin, 'A Family Shame: how did an alleged 'honour killing' take the lives of three sisters--weeks after they reached out for help?' in *Macleans* 124/43, November 7th, 2011

demonstrates the value and worth of women in a culture where women were treated poorly and often their testimony was dismissed. He also praised their service (Mark 14) and uses women as the key character in many of his parables (Luke 13:20-21, Luke 15:8-10). It is also a woman, Mary, who is the first person to see Jesus risen from the dead (John 20:11-18).

Jesus redefines adultery and divorce in Matthew 5:27-30, providing redemption for prostitutes and sinners (Luke 7:36-50) and vindicates monogamous marriage (Matt 19:3-12). He ate with, spoke with and spent time with women regularly (Luke 10:38-42) and showed compassion towards them, especially those who were considered 'sinful' by the rest of society (Luke 7:46-52). In the Sermon on the Mount, Jesus highlights one of the Ten Commandments which condemns murder redefining it to say those who remain angry at others are equally sinning. In other Scriptures, women are often mentioned in relation to cultural expectations, their role in relation to the body of Christ and also to marriage, women are encouraged to submit to their husbands as believers submit to Christ and men are told to love their wives as Christ loves the Church (Eph 5:22-23).

> *Succinctly one is a culture of forgiveness vs. a culture of blood revenge; one a culture of developing personhood vs a culture of control of women.*

Whilst there are similarities to the Qur'anic teachings, in that men must provide for their wives, there is little else the two texts have in common. Where one text depreciates the value of women in society and speaks of the intellect and witness of a woman being half (or even a quarter) that of a man's, the other speaks of unity and oneness in God (Galatians 3:28 – 'There is neither Jew nor Gentile, neither slave nor free, nor is there male or female, for you are all one in Christ Jesus.'). Whilst one speaks of admonishing and physically punishing your wife, the other speaks of loving and treating your wife as Christ treats the Church. Succinctly one is a culture of forgiveness vs. a culture of blood revenge; one a culture of developing personhood vs a culture of control of women. A Christian response to honour-based violence involves responding in anguish at the loss of life, longing for justice for those involved and praying for the conversion of the family that needs to seek forgiveness and be welcomed into the family of God.

A Conclusion

Honour killings are an all too prevalent issue amongst both Islamic Eastern and Western societies worldwide. Also we have discovered that the majority of honour crimes occur against women. It was

> *Honour killings are an all too prevalent issue amongst both Islamic Eastern and Western societies worldwide.*

significant; therefore, that we look at the Qur'anic and Biblical views on women and how this may affect an honour based culture and the prevalence of honour-based violence in these cultures. In light of this research and study, it is not difficult to see a correlation between Islamic teaching, the treatment of women and the act of honour killings predominately amongst Muslim communities. Put side by side with the biblical teachings of the value of women, forgiveness of the adulterer, the commandment not only to abstain from murder but also from unrighteous anger and to forgive, each religious teaching moves in a very different direction when it comes to the concept of honour. A Christian response to cases of honour killing is one of grief and urgency. Grief at the breaking of God's law by committing murder and grief at the attempt that is made to maintain a corrupted and unrighteous version of 'honour' through this. Honour can only be found in knowing and following Christ. A Christian response is also one of urgency; at the need to pray for and share the hope and forgiveness of Jesus Christ amongst communities where honour killings are taking place across the world.

Building Bridges through Stories

Macy Wong*
Student

Melbourne School of Theology

Shena is a woman from a Muslim people group in China. She works in a building complex and has the job of keeping an eye on the elevator in the surrounding buildings for six hours a day. If the elevator breaks, she calls someone to come and fix it. So as you can imagine, she has lots of free time. One day, she was approached and asked if she wanted to hear a story from the Bible. She said 'yes', so she heard the 'Creation' and 'Fall' stories. She was very keen to hear more, so for the next week Shena who was often joined by her son, met with the storyteller every day and they went through seven stories covering the whole story of the Bible. She started reading the Bible in her own language and listening to MP3's of a study specifically designed for Muslims. A few months later Shena started to dream about whether she should believe in Jesus, or Mohammed. Her son also built a relationship with the storyteller and one time they watched a version of the 'Jesus' film for children and he prayed at the end. The storyteller asked Shena's son if he believed in Jesus and he said he did.[1]

The ancient tool of storytelling was revived a few decades ago by Western missionaries and many are using various Bible story formats for evangelism and discipling to communicate the true revelation of God.[2] In order to help the listener find themselves in God's story and capture

> ... *many are using various Bible story formats for evangelism and discipling to communicate the true revelation of God.*

---

*Macy Wong is a pseudonym
[1] Story from a personal source
[2] Jack Colgate, (2008), "Relational Bible Storying and Scripture Use in Oral Muslim Contexts. Part 1," *International Journal of Frontier Missiology,* 25/3, 136.

their attention, the storyteller must be aware of potential barriers and build bridges through their chosen story. The above account is an example of contextualisation where the storyteller is an outsider who is seeking to communicate cross-culturally. "Contextualisation requires an exploration by outsiders into the insiders' world in order to discover those cultural elements that resonate with the message that they desire to communicate."[3]

> *God's message in the Bible is full of stories, so it is actually well-suited to be contextualised in an oral story format*

Contextualisation is considered to be crucial in relating the gospel to culture; however, there are many different approaches to contextualisation in mission to Muslims.[4] God's message in the Bible is full of stories, so it is actually well-suited to be contextualised in an oral story format. My aim is to focus on the contextualisation of God's word through a relational approach to Bible storytelling among Muslim people. In terms of contextualising the Bible stories, the storyteller needs to discover how a scriptural narrative resonates with the culture, in order to craft the story appropriately to provide impact.[5] However, there are practical considerations, including key themes that can be used in order to build bridges as well as some limitations so as to avoid barriers that might arise.

Back to Orality

"Orality" refers the reliance upon the spoken, rather than written, word for communication.[6] In the present age of biblical illiteracy, approximately 80% of the world does not seem to hear or understand the

> *In the present age of biblical illiteracy, approximately 80% of the world does not seem to hear or understand the message when communicated through literate ways and means*

---

[3] Mark Naylor, (2004), "*Towards Contextualized Bible Storying: Cultural Factors which Influence Impact in a Sindhi Context*" Master of Theology Thesis, University of South Africa, 14 http://uir.unisa.ac.za/bitstream/handle/10500/2060/dissertation.pdf?sequence=1 cited 8 July, 2104
[4] M. Coleman, & P. Verster, (2006), "Contextualisation of the Gospel Among Muslims," *Acta Theologica* 2 94.
http://www.ajol.info/index.php/actat/article/viewFile/49037/35385 cited 8 July, 2014
[5] Naylor, "*Towards Contextualized Bible Storying.*" 12.
[6] What is Orality? https://oralitystrategies.org/about.cfm cited 8 July, 2014

message when communicated through literate ways and means.[7] This is a huge concern, especially when approximately 90% of Christian missionaries working among the primarily auditory learners use literary-based communication styles.[8] No wonder there appears to be a growing movement among mission movements to return to Jesus' oral method of communication in order to win the oral majority (illiterate, functionally illiterate, or semi-literate).[9] A recent issue of the *International Journal of Frontier Missions* (IJFM), featuring the topic of 'Applied Orality: More than Methods', confirms the global resurgence of orality amongst oral preference learners, which has "tectonic implications for our stewardship of the gospel for this century."[10]

Charles Madinger describes orality in missions as "a complex of how oral cultures best receive, process, remember and replicate (pass on) news, important information, and truths."[11] Alex G. Smith identified five tools of oral communication: memory, repetition, storytelling, visual objects and the arts.[12] So although the Bible can be used among oral seekers and disciples of Jesus in other ways (a lectionary, a *kitab*[13] through which

> ... there appears to be a growing movement among mission movements to return to Jesus' oral method of communication in order to win the oral majority ...

---

[7] Ellen L. Marmon, (2013). "Teaching through the Lenses of Orality and Literacy: One Professor's Journey," *Religious Education: The Official Journal of the Religious Education Association* 108/3 312-327.
Grant Lovejoy, (2012). "The Extent of Orality 2012 Update," *Orality Journal* 1/1, 11-39.
[8] "Missions," *Touchstone: A Journal of Mere Christianity* 19/4 (2006), 49.
[9] Dawn Herzog Jewell, (2006), "Winning the Oral Majority," *Christianity Today* 50/3, 56.
[10] 'From Gutenberg to Zuckerberg', *Mission Frontiers* (May-June 2014), Pasadena: US Centre for World Missions
http://www.missionfrontiers.org/pdfs/36-3-MF_May-June_2014-full-Issue-web.pdf 4, cited 13 May 2014.
[11] Charles Madinger, (2010), "Coming to Terms with Orality: A Holistic Model," *Missiology* 38/2, 204.
[12] Alex G. Smith, (2008) "Communication and Continuity Through Oral Transmission," in *Communicating Christ Through Story and Song: Orality in Buddhist Contexts* ed. Paul H. De Neui; Pasadena, Ca: William Carey Library,. 11-12. Memory – where core facts, central beliefs and basic themes are consistent despite embellishments in details that appear over time, Repetition – reinforces communication and consolidates its transmission, Storytelling – Appears in different styles but is a powerful tool for effective communication of Christ to the nations (both literate and oral ones), Visual objects – Crests, symbols or totems are tangible references that tell silent stories, The arts - Songs, music, dance, and drama transmit messages in all cultures.
[13] *Kitab* is an Arabic word referring to a book.

God speaks, *kitab* of instruction, *kitab* of wisdom, songbook, prayerbook, source of creeds)[14], this essay will only focus on the tool of storytelling to Muslims.

Rationale for Storytelling to Muslims

The use of storytelling to reach Muslims is starting to gain widespread acceptance and adoption. Jack Colgate, who has lived among a Southeast Asian Muslim people group for over eighteen years, highlights at least two important reasons why we should use Bible stories in our gospel sowing and discipling among Muslims.

> *... well over half of the Bible is in narrative format with the remainder being teaching and meditative*

The first is that 71% of Muslim people groups have been found to have an oral rather than literate learning preference. That is they favour stories, parables, and formulaic sayings such as proverbs, symbols and dramatized dialogue.[15] Literate learners think in terms of information, propositional truth and order. Secondly, well over half of the Bible is in narrative format with the remainder being teaching and meditative.[16] "Narrative is the preferred genre of the biblical text...because the heart of the

> *Telling stories from the Bible encourages a use of the Scriptures that are predominantly already in narrative form.*

message of the Scriptures is itself the story of the redemptive plan of God."[17] Telling stories from the Bible encourages a use of the Scriptures that are predominantly already in narrative form. It also places God as the central character in contrast to the Prophet who is the focus of popular Muslim piety.[18]

---

[14] Jack Colgate, (2008), "Relational Bible Storying and Scripture Use in Oral Muslim Contexts. part 2", *International Journal of Frontier Missiology*, 25/4, 205.
[15] Results of the Global Trends and Fruitful Practices Consultation survey stated in Jack Colgate, "Bible Storying and Oral Use of the Scriptures," in *From Seed to Fruit: Global Trends, Fruitful Practices, and Emerging Issues among Muslims* (ed. John Dudley Woodberry; (2008) Pasadena, CA: William Carey Lib.), 220.
[16] Colgate, "Relational Bible Storying and Scripture Use in Oral Muslim Contexts. Part 1." 140.
[17] Walter C. Kaiser, Jr., (2003), *Preaching and Teaching from the Old Testament: A Guide for the Church*, Grand Rapids, Mich., Baker Academic, 63.
[18] "Muhammad," in *Encyclopaedia of Islam*, ed. P. Bearman, et al. (2014). Brill Online,

Storytelling takes into account the listeners' cultural, non-literary and orality preference, resistance to traditional gospel presentations, hostility, and other religion factors.[19] "The world's major religions are both propagated by stories and maintained by stories. These stories are most often told by leaders and attributed to their religion's founder or other ancestral teachers. Religious teaching in most societies is passed on through stories."[20] William A. Graham points out that "the spoken word of scripture has been overwhelmingly the most important medium through which religious persons and groups throughout history have known and interacted with scriptural texts".[21] Therefore, there is power in the 'telling' of Scripture in any situation or culture.

> ... there is power in the 'telling' of Scripture in any situation or culture.

Different Storying Methods

There are two main storying methods. Chronological Bible Storying (CBS) has been widely used since the 1980s. It is the process of encountering God by telling a chronological series of Bible stories without interruption or additional commentary.[22] Each telling is followed by a time of elicit discussion. CBS is used for evangelism, discipleship and church planting as it gives pre-literate people with no previous exposure to Christianity the necessary background to understand the concepts that lead up to the Gospels and Jesus' coming.[23]

Another effective way to tell stories is using a single Bible story to address a particular need, i.e. point-of-need Bible storying.[24] This kind of Bible storying method is less documented. However, it has

---

http://referenceworks.brillonline.com/search?s.q=muhammad&s.f.s2_parent=s.f.cluster.Encyclopaedia+of+Islam&search-go=Search cited 8 July, 2014.

[19] J. O. Terry, (2014) "Bible Storying Handbook for Short-Term Church Mission Teams and Mission Volunteers (Revised Edition)", https://oralitystrategies.org/resources.cfm?id=409,5 cited 13 May 2014.

[20] J. O. Terry,(2014) "Bible Storying Handbook for Short-Term Church Mission Teams and Mission Volunteers (Revised Edition)." 11.

[21] William A. Graham, (1987), *Beyond the Written Word: Oral Aspects of Scripture in the History of Religion*, Cambridge: Cambridge Uni. Press, 155.

[22] Many resources about CBS at https://oralitystrategies.org/strategies.cfm?st=1 cited 8 July, 2014.

[23] Don Fanning, (2009), "Chronological Bible Storying/Teaching, " *Themes of Theology that Impacts Missions.* Paper 6, p 3. http://digitalcommons.liberty.edu/cgm_theo/6, cited 8 July 2014.

[24] Colgate, "Bible Storying and Oral Use of the Scriptures." 222.

been found to be effective in Muslim cultures, particularly among women who tend to share stories of their personal misfortune and grief more openly than men.[25] It may also be wise to reserve stories involving Jews, the crucifixion and the resurrection until the person has become more mature in their faith so they can receive the stories without having a negative reaction due to an offending misunderstanding. These point-of-need stories can be easily prepared to address many troubling concerns and needs. Jack Colgate has suggested a module that includes stories and parables that portray the following: for example, God seeing and caring for the needy and poor; the danger of living in fear, panic, and jealousy; Good news for those who hide shame; the importance of forgiving others.[26] In order to tell single point-of-need stories we obviously need to be rooted in a deep, trusting relationship with our Muslim friends to know their personal stories and struggles.

A Relational Approach

Storytelling to Muslims works particularly well since it uses a relational approach rather than confrontational one as evaluated by Martin Jackson in "Missiological Approaches to Islam".[27] The relational approach is "central and essential to a theology of missions to Islam" and also "gives the scope for the development of a broad range of creative ways to engage with Muslims".[28] In some western contexts, the confrontational approach is important for those who specialise in lovingly defending Christianity against radical Islamic voices and holding Islam accountable for the actions of its followers. However, for the majority of Christ's followers, a relational approach is the only suitable and fruitful approach to adopt.

> *However, for the majority of Christ's followers, a relational approach is the only suitable and fruitful approach to adopt.*

---

[25] J. O. Terry, "Good News for Those with Stories of Grief: A Message for Women Who Share Stories of Personal Misfortune and Grief"
https://oralitystrategies.org/files/1/389/Stories%20of%20Sorrow%20an.pdf cited 13 May, 2014.
[26] Colgate, "Bible Storying and Oral Use of the Scriptures." 222-223
[27] Martin Jackson, (2009), "Missiological Approaches to Islam: Confrontational Versus Relational," *Australian Journal of Mission Studies*, December 31-38.
[28] Jackson, (2009) "Missiological Approaches to Islam: Confrontational Versus Relational." 36.

An example of a current ministry building relationships with Muslims is through SMILE (Supporting Migrants in Learning English). The group has been growing steadily in a small town in Western Australia over the past few years. (The increase of immigrants in this area is partly due to 'regional visas' which force settlement outside a major city). Through two SMILE groups which meet weekly (one for men, and one for women), a team of eight Christian volunteers has been able to build relationships with many immigrant families (mostly from Muslim backgrounds) in their region. The groups are primarily about support and friendship but also for English language practice. When the women meet, they often have cultural exchange in the form of a cooking class and the volunteers will tell point-of-need Bible stories whenever the opportunities arise. As well as their weekly group time, they visit their SMILE friends at home, drop off bread and make time to listen to their stories. This important groundwork has laid the foundations for introducing a Chronological Bible storying approach which they are planning to commence soon.

Practical Considerations: Bridges, Barriers and Limitations

Bridges
Miriam Adeney suggests that as stories are told, they must be communicated in the context of common themes: Muslim themes (e.g. circumcision, strong family ties), cultural themes (e.g. supernaturalism, communalism) and gender specific themes (e.g. women are vulnerable and multitask holistically).[29] Rick Brown has also identified ten Biblical themes that appeal to open-minded Muslims.[30] (See Appendix One for a list of themes). Focusing on the right themes can be used to build bridges and positively influence a person's consideration of the gospel. The storyteller needs to consider the worldview issues as well as doctrinal truths for salvation in order to decide which stories will most effectively target issues deemed significant to the listener and increase the spiritual interest and relevancy of Jesus as their saviour from sin.[31] When we are sensitive to cultural elements, we can discover the ways Bible narrative impacts the culture and recognise that God speaks to

---

[29] Miriam Adeney, (2002) *Daughters of Islam: Building Bridges with Muslim Women,* Downers Grove, Il. IVP, 61, 64, 156-158
[30] Rick Brown, (2007) "Biblical Muslims," *International Journal of Frontier Missiology* 24/2, 66.
[31] Grant Lovejoy et al., (2004), *Making Disciples of Oral Learners,* Pattaya, Thailand: Lausanne Committee for World Evangelization, 58

cultures in ways specific to their framework of understanding.[32] For example, the Muslim society operates out of an honour-shame framework, so they will be more sensitive to the concept of Jesus' removing our shame, than to the idea of Jesus removing our guilt.[33] In such a context, the greatest felt need is not salvation from sin but deliverance from defilement. For those who are dishonoured, sin is conquered by the restoration of honour.[34]

Bridges to friendship and engaging conversations can take place even during Ramadan, which usually poses a difficult time for Christians to engage Muslims in spiritual conversation, especially in relation to the Gospel.[35] Stories that could be used to build bridges during this time include: Jesus fasting in the desert (Matthew 4:1-11), the parable of the Great Banquet (Luke 14:15-24), Elijah and the widow (1 Kings 17:7-16).

Another type of 'bridge' is a 'door opener' involving differences which appeal to the audience and encourage them to open their hearts and minds to hear the message. An example for people who emphasize honour through vengeance is the story of Joseph forgiving his brothers. This presents a new value and a new concept of God when they realise that despite the bad things Joseph's brothers did, God was working in Joseph's life to bring out the good. This appeals to them and opens the door to share more of the Word.[36]

Barriers
"Barriers deal with the negative aspects of culture, religion, knowledge, interest, and other influences that hinder a listener in his hearing, understanding or acting upon the message of the gospel. These issues require a stories but with a different emphasis. That is stories that will disarm or demolish the negative aspects;

---

[32] Naylor, "Towards Contextualized Bible Storying." 18.
[33] Roland Muller, (2001). *Honor and Shame: Unlocking the Door*, Bloomington IN: Xlibris Corporation
[34] Bruce Sidebotham, "New Paradigm for Outreach to Mid-East Cultures: Gospel Restores Honor to the Dishonoreddefen
http://oprev.sidebotham.net/wp-content/back_issues/1stQtr02.htm#feature3, 1 cited 8 July, 2014.
[35] L.D. Waterman, (2014,) "A Survey of Ramadan's Effects on Muslims' Openness to the Gospel," *St Francis Magazine* April, 35.
[36] Lovejoy et al., *Making Disciples of Oral Learners*, 59.

qualify or otherwise nullify the barrier that cause hindrances".[37] Although stories can bypass the defence mechanism of those hostile to western or Christian teaching, we still need to be cautious about which topics to avoid when witnessing to Muslims.[38] If we are not aware of significant barriers such as, the divinity of Christ or the Trinity, our efforts may be ineffective and may close the door of opportunity to share more Bible stories. Some worldview issues can be better dealt with after the basis for a changed life has been established.

Limitations and Considerations
"Among the limitations of Bible Storying: It takes time, especially if many stories are used and the listeners are given an opportunity to participate in the storying session."[39] Regardless of which storytelling method is used, the desire is for the stories to be reproducible in order to facilitate the making of more disciples. However, church planter Christine Dillon noted that when she asked people to re-tell the stories to others, "people feel overwhelmed by the size of the task. For many of us, this is enough to prevent us from even making a start."[40]

> *The Bible stories must be crafted through cultural lenses without compromise to the original Scripture and only delivered after listening to the hearers' perspective*

Author-practitioners such as Colgate and Naylor argue from their experience that one can neither do CBS nor 'fire off' stories in the same way they would present propositional truths, like the 'Four Spiritual Laws'. Naylor asserts that "many applications of 'CBS' are often based upon western cultural and theological assumptions and, therefore, do not properly take into

---

[37] *Using Bridges and Barriers to Plan Stories*
https://oralitystrategies.org/strategies.cfm?st=1&id=16 cited 8 July, 2014.
[38] *When witnessing to Muslims... What to Avoid*
http://www.30-days.net/islam/howto/to-avoid/ cited 8 July, 2014.
[39] J. O. Terry and Daniel R. Sanchez, "Bible Storying Article 5: Limitations of Bible Storying",
http://www.bpnews.net/35181/bible-storying-article-5-limitations-of-bible-storying cited 8 July, 2014
[40] Christine Dillon, (2012), *Telling the Gospel through Story: Evangelism that Keeps Hearers Wanting More*, Downers Grove, IL., IVP, 47.

account the cultural setting of the listeners."[41] The Bible stories must be crafted through cultural lenses without compromise to the original Scripture and only delivered after listening to the hearers' perspective.

We need to be careful that we do not merely deliver curriculum content as stories in order to convert hard facts, but we must use the narrative to build a new worldview rooted in the Bible itself. Michael Goheen warned against fragmenting the Bible into bits – "moral bits, systematic-theology bits, devotional bits, historical-critical bits, narrative bits. When the Bible is broken up in this way there is no comprehensive grand narrative to withstand the power of the comprehensive humanist narrative that shapes our culture."[42] Although we may be limited by time, we need to ensure that individual stories are linked into their larger narrative.

Conclusion

In conclusion, no matter whether we are based in Asia or Australia, there is an inextricable link between story, relationships and worldview. Prayer is essential to undergird our use of story to build bridges with Muslims. The contextualisation of Bible stories is not just a tool. The true power of narrative can be embraced when we present the whole biblical story as the meta-narrative of reality. This is not only to displace the old worldview, but to build a worldview and transform people and communities.

According to Paul, faith comes from hearing the message (Romans 10:17). We must become powerful storytellers like Jesus and pass on important truths through stories. "The truth must be told with cultural sensitivity and in the preferred learning style of the people in order for them to grasp it."[43] Only then will the Good News resonate in Muslim hearts. In an increasingly print-dominated and literate western culture, it is our return to 'orality' and the oral use of Scriptures that offers hope for building bridges to Muslims.

---

[41] Mark Naylor, "Contextualized Bible Storying" http://www.nbseminary.ca/wp-content/uploads/Contextualized%20Bible%20Storying%20for%20EMS.pdf 2, cited 8 July, 2014.
[42] Michael W. Goheen, "The Power of the Gospel and the Renewal of Scholarship," http://www.biblicaltheology.ca/blue_files/Inaugural-Goheen.pdf , 5-6, cited 8 July 2014
[43] John Dudley Woodberry, (2008), *From Seed to Fruit: Global Trends, Fruitful Practices, and Emerging Issues among Muslims,* Pasadena, Ca.: William Carey Lib., 286.

Some Biblical Themes that Appeal to Muslims

(Adapted from 'Biblical Muslims' IJFM, page 66).

Qualities:	Demonstrated in the following books/stories:
God's goodness, love, reliability, and care for his servants	Abraham, Joseph, the Exodus, Daniel, Jesus, and the Apostles, among others
God's guidance of history towards good ends as he works through events to oppose evil, to train his servants in righteousness and truth, and to fulfil his good purposes for his people.	Abraham, Joseph, Moses, Ruth, David, Jonah, Daniel, Job, and in Revelation.
The portrait of Jesus himself: his kindness, devotion, wisdom, power, and ongoing reign as Saviour and King.	The Gospels
The love and forgiveness exhibited by true followers of Jesus.	Prescribed in the Gospels, particularly the Sermon on the Mount, and it can be seen in stories from the Acts of the Apostles and in the lives of true disciples that people meet today. A similar theme is present in the story of Joseph.
The offer of personal forgiveness and acceptance by God.	Gospels and in Acts.
The offer of assured and complete salvation from hell and acceptance into God's kingdom.	This is foretold in Isaiah 53, and developed in the Gospels, particularly in Matt. 11:27–29; Luke 7:36–50; 10:20; 12:32; 23:42–43; John 3:14–16; 11:25–27; 20:31.
The offer of a personal relationship with the Lord, fully realized in the next life.	Matt. 18:20; 28:20; John 14:16-20; Acts 18:10; Rev. 21–22.
The offer of inner cleansing and	Segments of the Gospels, Acts, and

renewal through God's Holy Spirit.	Epistles.
The offer and example of grace to live a godly life through the strengthening and guidance of the Holy Spirit.	Acts of the Apostles and in some of the Epistles
Power to resist and repel Satan and evil spirits in Jesus' name.	Found in the Gospels (e.g., Luke 10:17–20), Acts, James, 1 Peter.

Oh Christians, Leave our Lands!

Ahmad Al-Sarraf
Journalist

from *Al-Qabas Newspaper* (Kuwait), 21 July 2014[1]

> This is not the usual type of article printed in *The Bulletin*.
>
> The topic though (and you must read the article before you understand its point) is worthy of your attention. Please read it with care and withhold your judgment until the end.
>
> (Mary's Well, Occasional Papers)

O Christians of Damascus, Yabrud, and Ma'lula, leave our lands. Leave our countries, O Christians of Mosul, Nineveh, and Baghdad. Christians of Lebanon leave our mountains and valleys. O Christians of Palestine and the Gulf, leave our coasts and our heartlands. All of you, get out from under our skin! Leave, all of you, for we hate you and don't want you in our midst. Leave, for we have grown weary of progress and civilization, of openness and forgiveness, of love and brotherhood, of coexistence and tolerance. Leave us alone to kill one another.

Leave, for you are not of us, nor we of you. Leave, for we have tired of your original presence in Egypt, Iraq, Syria, and Palestine. Leave so that we need not be embarrassed in your presence when our eyes meet your eyes that question us, "What happened?" Get out and leave us to our calamities: You have

> *... we have grown weary of progress and civilization, of openness and forgiveness, of love and brotherhood, of coexistence and tolerance. Leave us alone to kill one another.*

whoever will take you in; we will stay here distant from you, from

---

[1] Also published in *Mary's Well Occasional Papers*, 3:2, August 2014, Nazareth Evangelical Theological Seminary, translated by NETS staff. Reprinted here by permission.

your claims, your giftings, your capacities, your science, and your experience.

Get out and leave us with fanaticism, animus, and hatred. Leave, for we can no longer bear that which you call civilization. Your departure will leave us free to excise it all and wipe out all traces of it and to shatter what statuary and deformities and traces your ancestors left behind in stone, poetry, prose, and literature. Leave, for neither Iraq nor Egypt, nor Syria nor Kuwait, nor Palestine nor Jordan, nor beautiful North Africa need you, nor of any of those who lived among us before you, whether Gypsies, Jews, or even stones.

Go and leave and take mercy away with you, for we, after the Nusra Front, and ISIS, and Al-Qaeda, and the gangs of the Muslim Brothers, and their latest offshoots--we no longer need mercy and compassion. No, blood will flow, and violence spread, and hearts break, and livers be eaten, tongues cut out, necks broken, and knees collapse. We will return to archaic medicine, herbal treatments, reading (only) the ancient texts, and reading fortunes in sand.[2]

Fly away, Oh Christians, and take with you all remains, and even the bones, of Jubran Jubran, Sarkun Boulos, Badawi al-Jabal, Anastasis the Carmelite, Yousef Sa'igh, Sa'idi al-Malah, and the sons of Taqla, and Yaziji, and Bustani, and Akhtal the Younger. Also take with you your universities and hospitals and close your missions. Don't forget to take Mikha'il Nu'ima—we have no need of him—neither forget Mayye Ziyada and the sons of Ma'louf, Sarouf, and the sons of Ghali, and Zaydan, Khazin, Bistros, Thabit, and Sakikini—All of these are not from us, nor we from them.[3]

Yes, flee from us for we want to return to our deserts, for we long for our swords and our dirt and our livestock. We don't need you, or your civilization, or your contributions in language and poetry, for we have that which fills the gap you leave, namely radical groups and killers and shedders of blood. Get out, Oh Christians,

---

[2] This refers to a magical practice of trying to read fortunes from patterns in sand.

[3] The author here lists several famous Arab Christian men and women of literature from the modern period. They contributed greatly to the national and literary "Arab Renaissance" of the 19th and 20th centuries.

with your culture, for we have substituted for it a culture of digging graves.

Translators' comments
This bold, courageous, and rhetorically powerful piece by a Muslim author appeared recently in a Kuwaiti newspaper. This work is indicative of the physical trauma, spiritual wrenching, and social morphing of the modern Middle East and Muslim world. In many respects, in terms of violence, oppression, and fanaticism, these days of Islamic resurgence are dark and horrific. On the other hand, against a field of deepest night, many lights are yet piercing the gloom. Many Muslims are recoiling from the destruction and hatred around them. Some, like this author, are courageously standing against the flood of violence and rejection.[4]

By the grace of God, in these painful times, may many eyes, minds, and hearts be opened.

---

[4] As people of the Gospel, as debtors to the grace of Jesus, we of all people must not reduce Muslims or anyone else to a two-dimensional construct, to sub-human caricatures. Muslims are people made in the image of the Father, made to know him.

Shari'a Finance Uncovered:
Ethical Finance but whose Ethics?

Vickie Janson
Victorian State Director
Australian Christians

British Newspaper, the Daily Mail, uncovered in July, 2013 that Senegalese Muslim footballer, Papiss Cisse, estimated to earn around £40,000 per week, was refusing to wear Newcastle United's branded training kit or match day shirt, because it is against his religious beliefs.

It appears that other Muslim Newcastle United players have not taken this stance toward donning a Wonga shirt, the payday loan firm that won the club's new sponsorship deal. But it appears Cisse has a greater commitment to Shari'a compliance than his co-religionists.

His refusal to wear the payday loan firm's insignia is based on his belief that Shari'a does not allow Muslims to benefit from lending money; that Shari'a compliance forbids interest to be paid on bank accounts or added to mortgages. Such a strong stand by Cisse may seem a little ironic given his willingness to wear the previous shirts sponsored by Virgin Money and his exorbitant salary, no doubt, being the product of the same interest bearing system he opposes.

> *"Such a strong stand by Cisse may seem a little ironic given his willingness to wear the previous shirts sponsored by Virgin Money and his exorbitant salary no doubt being the product of the same interest bearing system he opposes."*

However, with promises of no interest and the concept of ethical investment being hailed as the greatest selling feature of Islamic Shari'a finance in Australia, perhaps it is worth considering both those claims.

Shari'a compliant finance is simply finance that complies with Islamic Shari'a law. It is the financial arm of a foreign and religious body of law. This is the first important issue. In order to facilitate Shari'a finance locally, there must be legal compliance to a body of religious law that transcends national boundaries and commercial law, essentially deferring to the quasi state of Islam. Rather than simply offering another financial product, this unfortunately supports Islamist ideals and ultimately the concept of the Islamic Caliphate.

Indeed, the philosophical origins of Shari'a finance date back to the 1920's and the founder of the Muslim Brotherhood Hassan al-Banna. He promoted the concept of 'financial jihad' and the Muslim Brotherhood have promoted this as a means to erode western markets and economies; something that one would expect to be at odds with Australia's national interest. Chairing the 2002 Islamic Financial Services Board (IFSB) meeting, then Malaysian Prime Minister Mahathir Mohamad stated, 'A universal Islamic banking system is a jihad worth pursuing to abolish this slavery (to the West).'

The claim to being a means of ethical investment begs the question 'whose ethics?' One of the highest Shari'a finance regulatory bodies is the Bahrain based Accounting and Auditing Organization for Islamic Financial Institutions (AAOIFI). It is my understanding that Australia has adopted AAOIFI standards. However, AAOIFI International Chairman Mufti Taqi Usmani has also been accused of supporting violent jihad, promoting Shari'a law in the West, and running a Pakistani madrassa that has trained thousands of Taliban!

While Dow Jones no longer employs Usmani, he is still chairman of AAOIFI, the umbrella organization guiding Australian investment. It should not be surprising that Italian economist Loretta Napoleoni stated for Front Page magazine that 'Islamic Banks…are the life-line of Wahhabi insurgency, they are the feeder of Islamist armed groups, without them terror-donations could not reach the end users scattered around the world'.

However it's not just the alleged connection to terrorism that challenges the claims to ethical investment. Shari'a finance involves a theological proposition and at the heart of this is a doctrine that implies that the non-Muslim world, its people and systems, are unclean. Shari'a finance must be purified from all contamination - a term publicly promoted - and is done so by investment in Muslim-only charity. Most would agree that indiscriminate charity is more ethical than charity that discriminates against another person's belief or religion, viewing this as defilement. The values undergirding Shari'a ethics itself are not consistent with the UN Declaration of Human Rights, but rather reflect the Cairo Declaration of Human Rights subject to Shari'a law. The prohibitions against investment in the pork and hospitality industries merely boycott legitimate Australian industries and validate a belief that these are unethical in nature, as is the expectation of increased return on investment. Should our government acquiesce to this?

Perhaps the greatest consideration in promoting this financial product under the guise of being 'ethical' is the legitimacy of the claim that it is 'interest free'. As many Shari'a finance practitioners affirm, interest is merely rebadged as *fees, rental or profit*. According to Mahmoud ElGamal, Chair of Islamic Economics at Rice University in Texas USA, "All Islamic finance today is interest based". Islamic banking, merely 'Shari'a Arbitrage', is "first and foremost about religious identity".

Given this financial product is identity based, has philosophical origins intent on undermining Western interests, has been accused of sponsoring terrorism, discriminates against people in need of charity and legitimate Australian businesses, and veils the cost of banking by redefining interest, perhaps our government should consider, just as the UK Muslim footballer did, if this is an identity they wish to sponsor and wear.

Vickie Janson is a public speaker, human rights advocate and friend of the MST CSIOF. She has authored several books, 'Ideological Jihad' and 'Shari'a Finance: A Question of Ethics' and is the Victorian Senate Candidate for political party, 'Australian Christians'.

Communiqués

Allah, God, and the Trouble with Language

Brent Neely
Nazareth School of Theology

One flashpoint among many in the confused and often contentious interface between Christianity and Islam is the Arabic word most commonly used to refer to God. I am referring, of course, to the word "Allah." A frequent charge is that, as Christians, we ought not use this term because "Allah is the god of Islam, not of the Bible". Or, put even more tersely: "Allah is not God." However, if we take the simple statement, "Allah is not God," as a sufficient statement of the truth, we are leaving far too much unsaid. That simple phrase (Allah is not God) is too imprecise to be useful. That phrase may be expressing a zealous Christian sentiment, but it does not, I am afraid, represent sufficiently disciplined thinking.

Now, zeal based on understanding (*and rooted in love*) is surely a good thing. But the simple statement just articulated is not a fully grounded expression of truth. It does not adequately address the complex reality at stake in this point of contention between Christianity and Islam. The issue at stake is "Who is God, and what is he like?" With respect to this issue, further understanding is called for in our efforts to honour truth while loving God and others. I am convinced that the quintessential question is about the nature of God as Christians know him *versus* the way he is represented in Islamic thought. Unfortunately this central

> The problem is that the simple assertion (*Allah is not God*, or, *Allah is not the same as the God of the Bible*) obscures as much as it reveals.

question often gets "tripped up;" the conversation follows dead-end detours and founders on confusion and ambiguity over the Arabic word "Allah."

The problem is that the simple assertion (*Allah is not God*, or, *Allah is not the same as the God of the Bible*) obscures as much as it reveals. It covers over or ignores complex linguistic or historical realities--all the while purporting to present straightforward theological truth. But theological truth (speech about God) is not terribly useful, edifying, or even "truthful," unless couched in language and terms that are clear and responsibly deployed. That is, we cannot really sort out our theology until we have paid some attention to our word choice, to unpacking what we (and others) mean--and in other words, we cannot really address the *theology* of the statement in question (Allah is not God) until we have addressed the *language* involved.

The question of unpacking linguistic usage might apply even to the English term "God" itself (see quote from Barth below). We cannot assume that the English word comprised of the three letters "g", "o", and "d" works mechanically, automatically, and even magically in some way; it is unreasonable to assume that any person simply

> *Merely to say "God" in our modern, English speaking world is not to ensure that one has spoken truly and accurately of the God revealed to us in the Jesus of the Four Gospels.*

vocalizing the sound "*god*," must surely know, understand, and agree on the content to which the word "*god*" refers. Merely to say "God" in our modern, English speaking world is not to ensure that one has spoken truly and accurately of the God revealed to us in the Jesus of the Four Gospels. People may fill the term "God" with all sorts of varying and contradictory content; they do so all the time in fact, sometimes in the name of Christian faith, sometimes in explicit disavowal of faith. So much for the word "God." The issue becomes potentially even more acute when it comes to the term "Allah," not least because here we are working across a language barrier—speaking in English of an Arabic word. Once again, the problem is at least partly linguistic *before* it is theological. Certainly Allah is the name by which Muslims know "God" and by which he is allegedly revealed in the Qur'an. In antiquity, it seems too that

"Allah" was the chief god of the pre-Islamic pagan pantheon of some Arabs in the Arabian Peninsula.

However, there is more. As far as we can tell, "Allah" would also have been the term used by Arabic-speaking Christians *before Islam* for the God of the Bible. It surprises some to hear of Arabic-speaking Christians before Muhammad. Suffice it to say there were many before the Arabian "prophet" and there remain many today. That was then. What about now? Much the same still holds. Muslims refer to God as Allah. But, Arabic-speaking Christians do too. They have always done so. However one wishes to deal with the complex history of political, social, and religious influences on Arab culture, the fact remains that the Arabic lexicon is a given whether the person speaking the language is Muslim, Christian, or other. What I mean is, to a great degree*, the menu of word choices for someone speaking Arabic is the same whatever the faith of that person. And, in Arabic, the basic word for "God" is "Allah." If one wishes to communicate about God, including the Father of our Lord Jesus, in Arabic, one uses the term "Allah." All the honoured and established Arabic Bibles do the same. It is not a matter of choice or a matter of theology: to speak of God in Arabic is to use the term "Allah".

Do the Muslims claim primacy of place for "Allah" *as they understand him*? Obviously they do. But, despite appearances, despite the impact of the Qur'an, despite demographic superiority, Islam does not "own" the Arabic language. Nor does it "own" any people by rights; the God of Abraham, Isaac, and Jacob, the God of Messiah Jesus, claims all the nations. That one true God was praised in Arabic long before the rise of Muhammad, perhaps as far back as the birth of the church in Jerusalem at the feast of Pentecost (cf. Acts 2.11).

So, in reality, the "Allah-issue" is linguistic first, and only then is it theological. Once again, words are not magical entities freighted with mysterious essences. Even "sacred" names do not bear their precious truth *in isolation*. In other words, even special or spiritually significant names express their significance *only in a given context*. Take, for example, the name of God revealed in the Hebrew Scriptures, a name usually represented in English by the letters YHWH (archaically, "Jehovah") and often translated as LORD. Even the "name of God" does not bear its meaning suspended in a vacuum. It "means"--and we can appreciate what it "means"—only because YHWH has revealed himself in word and deed recorded in scripture. God himself has provided us with context, with a history of redemption, command, revelation, and faithfulness by which we might know the Lord (YHWH) himself.

Words, even names, are not meant to be used as "charms," at least not by the people of God. Take the example of the name "Jesus." This precious name of the beloved Son—it too was never meant to be exploited as a magical talisman, as if the name were a tool we could manipulate, *regardless of context or content*. See Acts 19.11-20. Context and content are vital to the meaning of "a name." It is never simply a question of the sounds formed when one voices certain letters in whatever language. Thus, in the case being discussed here, the sound "*Allah*" is not the issue. The question is, "What does that specific sound group refer to, and who decides?"

Words can carry multiple meanings and associations that shift over time and place. Their content is not eternally fixed; people disagree over the meaning or content of words, names, and terms all the time. Words are signs which point to meaning and significance *within given contexts*. For example, to use an English illustration; if an English-speaking Christian says the word "God" she surely is not meaning precisely the same thing as when an English-speaking Buddhist says the very same word. Thus, to communicate truly about God will require precisely *that*: a long, patient *communication* of the meaning, significance, and "person" we mean to refer to when we speak of "God". Just uttering the word (or forbidding the word, for that matter) will not advance the discussion much! So too when it comes to "Allah". It is rather fruitless to debate whether we can/should use the word "Allah". In Arabic, at least, one does not really have other good options. We dare not surrender the Arab world or the Arabic language to "other gods". Instead of abandoning Arabic we ought rather to claim that beautiful tongue for Jesus. The dispute really is not over whether to say "Allah." Arabic Christian worship has always praised God precisely with this term. The issue is not the word, but the meaning, the significance, the content.

For just a moment, let us divert to another example of a name that might have been made into a controversy, but apparently wasn't. Paul the Apostle shows no hesitation at all in using the given Greek name of his faithful friend and fellow minister, Epaphroditus (Phil. 2.25), even though the name originally was in honor of the Greek goddess Aphrodite. Epaphroditus - name, culture, background, and all - had been reclaimed and remade in Christ. The Greek name did not have to be abandoned. (Similar things might be said of the early church evangelist Apollos.)

My contention here is that we ought not to hand over meaningful speech about God ("Allah") in Arabic to the exclusive custody of Islam, as if signing away Jesus' claims on Arabic-speakers. Indeed, we cannot. Let us not surrender "the wealth of Egypt" to others, but let us rather, like the children of Israel, despoil Egypt of her treasures for the glory of the God of the Exodus. Let Arabic not be handed over wholesale to the proclamation of Muhammad, but let it join the chorus of multiple tribes, nations, and *tongues* glorifying the Father through Jesus the Lamb slain for the world.

Muslims and Christians both agree there is only one God, period. In the Arab world to say "God" one says "Allah." The real question then is not names (Allah); nor math (1 and only 1); but *identity*. Who is this one God? What is he like? How can we know him? And here we can respond with confidence, grace, faith, and humility: this God is the one revealed as our Saviour in the Bible, ultimately in Jesus from Nazareth who brings us home to the Father. *That* is what Allah is like. *That* is who he is. And there, in Jesus, and nowhere else, will you find him.

----

* There are, of course, various Arabic dialects. There are also some theological words, terms, and names that are typically either "Christian" or "Muslim." However, when it comes to the basic term for God, the one word, "Allah," is quite universal.

Postscript

On the topic of the meaning of "God," I want to provide the following sentence to give some context to a quote from Karl Barth relating to the word "God." Christians are those who navigate the treacherous seas of life invoking, praising, singing, thanking, and serving the one God whom they know as Father, through Jesus Christ.

They do not do this with the claim that of themselves they know better than everyone else. They do not do it as those who, on the grounds of their religion and tradition, in their kerygma and dogma, in their special theology and philosophy, offer to all the others a patent solution on a platter, who carry off the prize amid so much authentic and inauthentic certainty and uncertainty, so much imaginative and unimaginative fantasy, so many areas full or free of problems, so many necessary and unnecessary conflicts and compromises on the part of those who think and utter the word "God." Christians know that they are in too great solidarity with all other men not to have to admit that even when they think and utter it, the word "God" will always need afresh the genuine precision, fullness, and interpretation that come to it. And they know much too much about the one true and real God not to be clear that authentic interpretation cannot come to the word "God" by any human defining, meditating, or speculating--not even their own--but comes only when the Word of God aids the intrinsically impotent word "God" and gives it the only possible and correct content.

Karl Barth, *The Christian Life;* Church Dogmatics IV, *4; Lecture Fragments,* G.W. Bromiley, trans. (Grand Rapids, MI: Eerdmans, 1981), p. 54.

Egypt's Revolution II (July 2013)

Anonymous

The media, government spokespeople and hundreds of commentators had a field day reporting on and analysing the July 2013 deposing of President Morsi by the Egyptian military. Much was made of the unseating of Egypt's first democratically elected president in free and fair elections.

But were the 2012 elections free and fair? If we classify those elections as free and fair, it calls into question whether 'free and fair' is a good definition for defining whether an election truly expresses the will of the people. Morsi and the Muslim Brotherhood were elected on 15 million votes from a population of 85 million, and with an unprepared opposition, an alliance with far right fundamentalists, financial incentives and the compelling argument among the less educated that a vote against them was a vote against Islam, they won office. The situation is more complex than this, but the absence to foreign observers of obvious intimidation or irregularities on Election Day does not necessarily constitute 'free and fair' elections.

Upon winning power the Muslim Brotherhood largely abandoned democratic principles beyond the ballot box and immediately embarked on their Islamist agenda instead of tackling issues important to the lives of everyday people, surprising even many of their supporters who thought this would be a much more subtle process. They hijacked the constitutional process and pushed through a new constitution that most people hadn't read or understood, but which enshrined Shari'a law and discriminated against everyone except Islamists. Morsi then passed laws which put his personal decisions above the law and concentrated more power in himself than even Mubarak had, earning him the derogatory title, 'Pharaoh'. His administration began introducing Islamist social laws which were embarrassingly pointless at best or openly discriminatory at worst while ignoring pressing needs. He appointed ministers who were experts in Islamic law but had little experience in running a country with the problems facing Egypt and even less ability and interest in engaging with the world. For example, the IMF drew up a program for economic recovery which they would not or could not engage with, resulting in increasing poverty, power cuts, petrol queues, and a sharp decline in the currency. Foreign investment virtually ceased and thousands of companies left. Furthermore, they began open engagement with Hamas, the Syrian rebels and other terrorist groups in the region, frightening their neighbours and previous allies, including Egypt's own army which did not want radicals challenging Egypt's stability in the future or a confrontation with neighbours.

In early June 2013, opposition groups got together and planned to (a) collect more signatures than the number of votes which voted Morsi in, calling on him to resign and call early elections and (b) stage a demonstration on 30th June to mark one year in office and to present these signatures to the government. Twenty-two million signatures were collected on street corners, in packed train carriages, and in the markets. Banners and graffiti appeared everywhere; usually simply saying '30/6 Get out'. No one knew how successful this action might be.

On the 30th June, crowds far bigger than the demonstrations that brought down Mubarak gathered at Tahrir Square in the city centre and near the presidential palace in a northern suburb of Cairo. The atmosphere amongst the demonstrators was festive and peaceful. During those days, Human Rights Watch, though, documented over 100 rapes of women in the crowds carried out by Islamists, sent out in gangs of 20 men to surround and punish women for not staying at home.

Few had imagined the scale of support that the movement had mobilised. But the real surprise was the open support from the army and police that quickly became obvious. The demonstrations were a gift for both institutions. After the fall of Mubarak, the new government and the people had sidelined the police for their previous brutality. By supporting the demonstrations and refusing to protect Muslim Brotherhood property, the police were instantly brought back into the fold of society, suddenly finding themselves arm-in-arm with the people. The army, increasingly alarmed by the Muslim Brotherhood's erratic and dangerous foreign policy and its attempts to diminish the military's independence and economic empire now had a popular uprising it could buy into. Air force helicopters began to fly over the crowds of Cairo with huge Egyptian flags flying underneath them, all to wild applause by the crowds. After only two days, the military issued an ultimatum to Morsi that they would intervene if he didn't respond to the will of the people within 48 hours. There was an ecstatic atmosphere all over the city. "The army has rescued us", people said, and banners and flags began to appear everywhere simply with '48 hours'.

However, Morsi stuck to the line that he was the legitimate leader, offering a few concessions which were rejected by most people. True to their word, in a little over 48 hours, the army had deposed him.

In many ways, the Morsi administration was doomed from the outset. The military and police had spent the last 40 years trying to crush the Muslim Brotherhood and were in no frame of mind to cooperate with their newly elected enemies right from the start. No government can effectively rule without the cooperation of the police and military and for two years the police had not policed and the army did its own thing. Furthermore, the Muslim Brotherhood's lack of negotiating skills and determination to create an Islamist Egypt to the detriment of the economy and national security left the administration without the force it needed to ensure stability.

The military genuinely have no desire to run the country. Their experience in the period between the toppling of Mubarak and the June 2012 elections was not a good one. While February 2011 headlines around the world cry foul about the failure of Egypt's 'experiment with democracy', for Egyptians it's more about the failure of Egypt's experiment with Islamism. Furthermore, the people of the Middle East don't strive for democracy per se – what they want is freedom and justice. The Muslim Brotherhood knows this – the official name of their party is actually the Freedom and Justice Party. But as everyone who works in the Middle East knows, what is understood by such terms here is often very different from how people in the West understand them.

> *Egypt is now in a phase of deep division which started long before these recent events. Muslims, including those who voted for Morsi in the first elections, never imagined how divisive to society an Islamist government would become.*

One of the most moving scenes of these events was the Coptic Pope standing alongside the Grand Sheikh of Al Azhar University (the arbiter of Sunni Muslim law, amongst other things) with the military chief addressing the Egyptian people regarding the coup. Christian leaders are almost never given the opportunity for public exposure like this. Christians heaved a huge sigh of relief, the symbolism of this event revealing that many Egyptians, even important Muslims, do have a vision for a pluralist society.

Questions about what it means to be Muslim are on everyone's lips. Egypt now faces great uncertainty, but we know that God has often used social and political upheavals to grow His kingdom.

The Church's R2P

Elizabeth Kendal
Adjunct Research Fellow at the CSIOF,
Director of Advocacy,
Christian Faith and Freedom.

Responsibility to Protect, or R2P, is a United Nations [UN] initiative that encourages independent states to see sovereignty *not as a right* that allows them to act however they please within their own borders, *but as a responsibility*. It comes in response to increasing levels of violence within, as distinct from between, states.

Much of this violence is either sectarian (as in Syria, Iraq, Pakistan) or is greed based but fuelled by ethnic-religious hatred (as in Kachin State, Burma; the Nuba Mountains, Sudan; Papua, Indonesia). In each of the above cases, Christians are facing extreme persecution, even genocide.

It is no accident that religious violence has escalated markedly over recent decades. Trends such as the emergence of religious nationalism, the revival of fundamentalist Islam, the advance of cultural Marxism and the loss of Western influence have converged with the trends of massive population growth, rapid urbanisation and mass migration to create what analyst Gregory Copley describes as "a perfect strategic storm".

The US International Religious Freedom Act of Nov 1998 was a direct response to escalating religious persecution. But the economic crisis of late 2008 ripped the teeth out of the Act and now persecution with impunity is the order of the day. To use Isaiah's imagery, the Church is facing a mighty "flood" of persecution.

Christians across the Western world are largely oblivious to all this; partly because their churches (in general) are addicted to entertainment and/or they are living in denial and/or they are cruising along with an erroneous view of persecution which they regard as something one might learn about in a Church History course.

I am absolutely convinced that most Western Christians, including many church leaders, view the subject of persecution as irrelevant to Western Christians.

This is not inconsequential!

Firstly: the believer who regards another Christian's suffering as "not my concern" or "not something I want to be burdened with" has rejected (albeit subconsciously) the theology of our union with Christ along with the teaching that the Church is the family and body of Christ. Such an attitude not only grieves the Lord, it can lead to judgment (Ezekiel 34, Matt 25:41-45).

Secondly: persecution is stirring in the West on account of *Culture Change* which is driven by cultural Marxism's promotion of moral and cultural relativism. A godless, essentially Marxist state ideology is being imposed at the cost of religious freedom. Is the church prepared?

Jesus warned us that persecution would come (John 15:18 to 16:4) so that in being prepared, we would endure. Yet I would suggest that the church, in general, is not prepared and that many believers and churches will struggle to endure. There will be "shipwrecks", with many believers battered and many passengers lost at sea at a time when the world needs Christians to be firm in faith, exalting the Lord.

We need to stop watching believers and churches sailing into the future unprepared. Our cruising days are over! Much needs to be done to awaken the church and prepare her to face the storms ahead. Christian pastors, teachers and leaders must see this as part of their R2P!

The Legacy of the Mughals: from a Sikh Perspective[1]

Paragat Singh and Palbinder Singh
Researchers

A recent exhibition at the British Library on 'Mughal India', asserted that the Mughals ruled 'tolerantly' in South Asia from 1526. Any Sikh or indeed any reasonably well-informed English Christian knows that this is nonsense.

There were ten Sikh Gurus, spanning a consecutive period of 239 years from the advent of Guru Nanak in 1469, until the demise of Guru Gobind Singh in 1708, a period of time coinciding with the reigns of the 'great eight' Mughal Emperors.[2] Here we identify the differences in outlook that led to the conflicts between the House of Baba, the Sikh Gurus, and the House of Babur, the Muslim Mughals.

The Sikh Gurus introduced a new order, which identified the Divine at the epicentre of all human activity, including socio-political life. Sikhism is a philosophy which aims to reunite the human soul with the Divine soul by seeking to improve global society. The Sikh Gurus directly challenged violations of human rights, state oppression, religious bigotry and extremism.

Following the invasion of India by Babur, the first Mughal Emperor, Shari'a Law was introduced in India from about 1526 which would impinge adversely upon the other two major religions in India: Hinduism and Sikhism. Any religious ideology that would terrorise and degrade humans into slavery was contested by Guru Nanak. The dichotomy was between the rigid rules based on

---

[1] This article was first published in the Salisbury Review

Ed: *The founder of the Sikh religion was Guru Nanak (1469-1539). A guru in Sanskrit is considered 'an enlightened one, saint, teacher' though for the Sikhs it refers to those who were 'entrusted with divine enlightenment.' The word 'Sikh' means 'disciple'. Guru Nanak was followed by nine other Gurus, many of whom added further teaching and practice to the religion. Originally the Gurus announced their successor. The tenth Guru, Guru Gobind Singh, established Sri Guru Granth Sahib as the Sikh scriptures, which is considered the last and living guru. The Sikh place of worship is called a Gurdwara. .*

descriptive instructions of the Muslim Mughals and the flexible rule based on principles of enlightenment of the Gurus. Guru Nanak described the political context of the time in his hymns, a form of Gurbani poetry as "a darkened age where falsehood has triumphed over truth and where the instruments of state power are butchering their own citizens" The global vision of Guru Nanak favoured a non-sectarian, tolerant and plural society; a free and fair society enshrined with universal human rights. Guru Nanak rejected the claims that any faith had a monopoly of truth: "it was the deed and not the creed that mattered".

The Mughal Programme

In direct conflict with these fundamental Sikh precepts, the Islamic Mughals propagated the idea that it was the creed and not the deed that was paramount. Anyone in India who challenged the Shari'a laws would suffer death. Non-Muslims were subject to 'jizya' tax, and there was a Hindu pilgrimage tax. Indians were disempowered and reduced to slavery. The Mughals wanted to eliminate Sikhism by converting the Sikh Gurus to Islam. The Sikh Guru Nanak visited Islamic institutions at Mecca, Medina and Baghdad, where he confronted the most senior Muslim leaders on their failure to respect human rights. He questioned critically their concept of the ideal Muslim and how such people should act.

The Hindu situation

Owing to the Hindu caste-system, the Hindu use of entangling rituals, and their tendency to appeasement, the Hindus were unable to champion equality or social rights. However all forms of oppression were challenged by the Sikh Gurus and any religious justification for such oppression was rejected. Guru Nanak criticised the lack of any proper Hindu resistance to Islamic rule. Guru Nanak attended the elite Hindu institutions at Hardwar and the Himalayas where he discussed human rights with several Hindu saints. He strongly rebuked them for not safeguarding the masses from the Mughal onslaught. As the common man became increasingly inspired by the egalitarian teachings of Nanak, the Hindu priestly caste, the Brahmins, lost credibility among those they purported to lead. In response to this threat, the Brahmins complained about the Sikhs to their Mughal overlords and for reasons of self-interest became in effect allies to the Islamic State. Throughout the centuries of Mughal rule in India, many higher caste Hindus supported the Mughals.

The Sikh World-View

In his hymns, Guru Nanak outlined two key concepts that formed the basis of human response to any given situation.

"The first is that the evil, unless resisted grows and endures and does not wither away or die by itself ....The evil, therefore, must be resisted by human effort and destroyed .... But the evil must not be left alone till God on High chooses to intervene to destroy it.[3]"

It was this teaching which changed the entire attitude of the Sikh community to the onslaught of Islam in India.

Sikh Tolerance and Muslim Intolerance

It was the Guru Arjan, the 5th Sikh Guru (1563-1606), who composed the Sikh scripture, the *Guru Granth Sahib*. He was the author of a hymn that was severely critical of Islamic behaviour. This attracted a death penalty in accordance with Shari'a Law and he was burnt alive for refusing to embrace Islam. Prior to his death, he sent a message to the 6th Guru, the saintly Guru Hargobind (1595-1644) telling him he must now act like a sovereign. Hargobind was instructed to wear two swords to represent spiritual and temporal power. In response, the Islamic state decreed that a non-Muslim could not conduct any activity that reflected sovereignty; no non-Muslim might wear a turban, carry a sword, ride a horse, erect a throne higher than twelve foot or sing their own scriptures in public. Guru Hargobind rejected this totalitarian view. He was arrested by the state for defending the right of individuals to choose their own way of life. When imprisoned, he ordered his Sikh followers not to pay any fine demanded for his release, as this would give legitimacy to the legality of his detention. After his release the Emperor Shah Jahan on four separate occasions declared jihad on Guru Hargobind, but Guru Hargobind successfully defended his people and principles on the battlefield. Despite winning those battles, Hargobind did not seek to lay claim to any territory. But he had taught and empowered the Sikhs to

---

[3] Adapted from 7 Contributions of Guru Nanak, ed. Dr. M. Harnam Singh Shan, p 15,16 at http://archive.org/stream/ContributionsOfGuruNanakKapurSingh/Contributions%20of%20Guru%20Nanak%20-%20Kapur%20Singh_djvu.txt cited on 23 October, 2014.

defend human rights from oppressive regimes even if this meant, in the last resort, taking part in an armed conflict.

In 1675, Guru Tegh Bahadur, the 9th Guru of the Sikhs (1621-1675) received a deputation of Brahmins who petitioned him that the Emperor was planning to liquidate the non-Islamic population of India and would do so, unless a nobleman was prepared to defend them. The Emperor Aurangzeb gave the Guru an ultimatum: convert to Islam or face public execution. Guru Tegh Bahadur refused to convert to Islam and chose to challenge the entire legitimacy of this attempt at the Islamisation of India. Aurangzeb ordered the execution of Guru Tegh according to the basic state-laws of Islam.

The Sikh Legacy

The 10th Guru of the Sikhs, Guru Gobind Singh (1666-1708), was subjected to ferocious attacks throughout his entire life. The Muslims' principal aim was to eliminate Guru Gobind Singh. Despite suffering the loss of his parents, all his children and comrades, he refused to compromise or submit to oppression. In 1699, Guru Gobind Singh established the Order of the Khalsa, a fraternal and democratic order, to campaign and fight for human truths and freedom. In 1708, Guru Gobind Singh appointed Banda Singh the first Commander-in-Chief of the Sikhs to continue the fight against Islamic oppression. This is what really happened.

Contrary to what was suggested by the British Library exhibition, possibly to appease British Muslims, there is overwhelming evidence that the Mughals would not tolerate any difference from, or challenge to Islam. The Sikh Gurus' attempts to introduce notions of tolerance and equality were met with barbaric punishment from several Mughal emperors. The Mughals were quite unable to accept the existence and ideology of the Sikh Gurus. We have no reason to take seriously the thesis of Mughal tolerance propounded by the British Library in their exhibition.

Christian-Muslim Relations:
A Bibliographical History

Ruth Nicholls
Adjunct Research Fellow
Centre for the Study of Islam and Other Faiths.

How did early and modern Christians and Muslims in the South East Asian region relate to one another throughout history and, in their writings about one another? Did they rely on inherited stereotypes or move beyond them?

This question is central to one of the largest research projects that has ever been conducted into the history of Christian-Muslim Relations. The project aims to be "an exhaustive account of Christian-Muslim interaction through history" throughout the world for the period 600AD to 1900AD. The project, hosted at the University of Birmingham in the UK, funded by the British Arts & Humanities Research Council and published by Brill Publishers of the Netherlands is a multi-volume bibliographic history project called '*CMR1900*' for short. Currently six volumes have already been published.

For the purposes of this research project, the world has been divided into five regions: Western Europe, Eastern Europe, Middle East and North Africa, Asia and Oceania, and Africa and the Americas. MST's own Dr Peter Riddell, Director of the CSIOF, is leading a team of researchers for the South East Asian sub-region, of Asia and Oceania covering Burma, Thailand, Laos, Cambodia, Vietnam, the Philippines, Brunei, Malaysia, Singapore, and Indonesia. Together with assistance from CSIOF Adjunct Research Fellow Dr Ruth Nicholls and a team of volunteer researchers, Dr Riddell is attempting to compile an exhaustive list of works relating to Christian-Muslim Relations within this South East Asian region. CSIOF PhD candidate Denis Savelyev is also involved in the Eastern Europe regional team for this project.

"Both Islam and Christianity are 'imports' to the Southeast Asian region. Both have come with traders and both have sent their 'missionaries' and have interacted with each other in the region on the basis of a prior understanding of each other," Dr Riddell said.

Dr Nicholls added: "Finding original materials within the region, especially since local languages are also involved, is not an easy task. Currently our research team is investigating what is known as 'secondary' sources, which, we hope, will direct them to original writings or speeches in the original language of that area.

"On one level, modern technology makes the task a little easier because the internet makes it possible to search various library holdings for books, articles, pamphlets and newspaper reports which may refer to an original work or may report a speech or conversation."

Dr Riddell summed up the importance of involvement in the project in saying "I believe it is important that Christians, with a living faith, are involved in such research projects, rather than leaving it to secular institutions, so we can better understand missionaries in past centuries, and how they have contributed to modern Christian-Muslim relations."

Tomé Pires
A Portuguese traveller's reaction to encountering Islam

Ruth Nicholls
Adjunct Research Fellow
Centre for the Study of Islam and Other Faiths.

> CSIOF's Peter Riddell and Ruth Nicholls are involved in the University of Birmingham's project known as Christian-Muslim Relations: A Bibliographical History (see previous article). As part of that project, Ruth Nicholls was commissioned to research the writings of the Portuguese traveller Tomé Pires who encountered Muslims in Asia in the early 1500s. As a Portuguese he was aware of the struggle his country had faced in freeing itself from Islamic control. He was also a Catholic who was experiencing the growth and rise of Portugal as a significant political power. What follows briefly highlights the main thrust of what he wrote in his book *The Suma Oriental of Tomé Pires, An account of the East, from the Red Sea to Japan*, written in Malacca and India between 1512-1515.

Introducing Tomé Pires
It's about 1468. In Portugal, Tomé Pires is born into a Lusitanian family – possibly pointing to a heritage dating back to about 400BC when the Lusitanians, an early Celtic group, began settling in the Iberian Peninsula. During the Roman period the Peninsular was referred to as Hispania, a country the Apostle Paul desired to visit. There is a tradition that he did and some would mark the place on the coast.

Portugal and Islam
In the early eighth century, Berbers from North Africa with the help of some Arabs, known in the area as the Moors, conquered the Iberian Peninsula, claiming it for Islam. They were not able to take

an area on the north Atlantic coast, the Asturias. It was essentially from this kingdom that the Peninsula was won back from the Moors though it took many centuries. About a century later, the first Portugal county was formed following the re-conquest of the area from the Moors so that in 925 Ramiro II took the title of King of Portuguese land. Then, in 1065 Portugal was proclaimed an independent kingdom under Christian rule, having been freed from Moorish overlords. The eleventh century saw many fluctuations in the location of borders between Christians and Muslims. But by 1139 King Afonso I of Portugal declared himself vassal to Pope Innocent II, placing the Kingdom of Portugal and himself under the protection of Saint Peter and the Holy See. In 1147, the Moorish city of Lisbon fell to the King of Portugal with the help of Crusaders who during their ransacking and plundering of the city killed many Muslims. In 1179 Pope Alexander III, in a Papal bull, recognized Portugal as an independent country with the right to conquer lands from the Moors. With this papal blessing, Portugal was at last secured as a country and safe from any other 'Christian' attempts of annexation. By 1212 much of the western area of the Penninsular had been won back from the Moors so that in 1255, Lisbon became the capital of Portugal. In 1272 Portugal conquered the last Moorish stronghold and Islam was no longer a force in the country. (In Spain the process was much longer). Come the 16th Century Portuguese political power and seafaring skills had become strong and the Portuguese extended their rule and their territories to many parts of the world.

Pires' travels

So this was the historical context into which Tomé Pires was born. Following his father's trade the young Pires also became an apothecary to the royal household. Whether Pires was excited by the tales of the East that were coming into the court we do not know but with the approval of the King, he left Portugal in 1511 bound for the East as the 'factor of drugs'. Pires travelled from Egypt (the Red Sea) following the coast to India. His journey continued around the coast till he reached Malacca. From there Pires also sailed around the islands known today as Indonesia. The account of these travels forms 'books' in his work *Suma Oriental* [1] which he wrote between 1511 and 1515.

---

[1] *The Suma Oriental of Tomé Pires, An account of the East, from the Red Sea to Japan, Written in Malacca and India in 1512-1515, and The Book of Francisco Rodrigues, Rutter of a voyage in the Red*

This work is divided into six books; the first five deal with his travels while the sixth book focuses on the history of Malacca and especially its fall to the Portuguese. It would appear that he was commissioned to write reports of his journey. His writing concentrated on trade and its possibilities while also providing a wealth of information about harbours, sailing vessels, customs, and peoples. It also gives an insight into what a Portuguese Catholic of that period thought about Islam and the role that Portugal was playing in the expansion of Christianity.

The expansion of Catholic Christianity
What follows are some of his comments. Not surprisingly in the introduction to his work Pires described the 'Portuguese King as ruler whose dominions are the greatest stretching from Africa to China ... with an infinity of islands'. He also speaks of the Portuguese as 'carrying [the king's] banners into their lands in the name of our Lord Jesus Christ.' Pires continues:

> *All this is caused by Your Highness' great power here, which is exercised by the most magnificent and exalted knight Afonso de Albuquerque, your Captain-General, who is brave, astute and provident in war and .... Who never ceases her (Portugal) labours, fighting continuously now in High India, and now in Arabia, and in the midst of it all he never ceases fighting against the name of Muhammed (Mafamede). It is clear that God's omnipotence is favouring these efforts because He wills to make Christianity take root throughout your kingdoms, and that these things are accomplished by an immense expenditure of money such as no Christian King has ever made before, because they are never ceasing; yet it must all be considered money well spent because it is a thing which so exalts, increases and augments our holy Catholic faith, bringing such humiliation, loss and damage to the false diabolic opinion of the abominable, ignominious, false Muhammed, the head of the vain Moorish religious, that Your Highness has gained great fame and honour among princes in this world and infinite merit before the Most High God...(p2)[2]*

Sea, Nautical Rules, Almanack and Maps, Written and Drawn in the East Before 1515, translated from the Portuguese MS in the Bibliothèque de la Chambre des Députés, Paris, and edited by Armando Cortesão, works issued by the Hakluyt Society, reproduced by permission of the Hakluyt Society from the edition originally published by the Society in 1944, Kraus Reprint Limited Nendeln/Liechenstein 1967

[2] The page numbers refer to the location in the edition of the Suma mentioned above.

The Will of God

So Pires set the scene. To him, the expansion of Christianity, despite the cost, was an expression of God's power triumphing over the falseness of the Islamic religion. At the same time, while acknowledging that Portuguese triumph was a sovereign act of God, the tone, at least to modern ears, seems almost vindictive. These themes occur throughout his Suma as the following quotes reveal.

> *Goa was preparing to inflict great losses on the Christians, but God's judgment turned the loss upon them, for there is no doubt that the Moors groaned when Goa was taken* (p56).
>
> *The judgment of our Lord is incomprehensible, and let everyone take good note that the Moors suffered ... a greater loss in Goa than they will suffer when they lose Aden* (p56/57). ...
>
> *It is our Lord who decrees the downfall of Muhammed. ...*(p57)
>
> *The city of Goa is as strong as Rhodes. It has four fortresses, very richly constructed, in the necessary places, to injure the name of Muhammed.* (p58)

These attitudes are perhaps best reflected in his documentation of the fall of Malacca to the Portuguese:

> *However, the levity of the Malayans, and the reckless vanity and arrogant advice of the Javanese*[3] *and the king's (Malacca) presumption and obstinate, luxurious, tyrannical and haughty disposition-because our Lord had ordained that he should pay for the great treason he had committed against our people- all this together made him refuse the desire for peace* (p280).
>
> *And there is no doubt that this was the finest fleet that Portuguese ever saw in India, or with so many important people; and they [the Muslim forces] were still more heavily defeated, for which Our Lord*

---

[3] The history of South Asia includes the rise and fall of kingdoms. Inter-relationships between these kingdoms were primarily based on intermarriage, trade and also religion. So when Malacca decided to withstand the Portuguese, Malacca's allies gave their support.

be ever praised, for such a feat is not in our hands. And because Our Lord is not slow with His justice, the people of Java were tamed, and those of Palembang who came with Pate Unus killed, at which Guste Pate of Java and the lord of Tuban [Indonesia] were not all displeased (p282).[4]

The Kashises[5] and their mollahs telling him that he should not make peace; for as India was already in the hands of the Portuguese, Malacca should not pass to the infidels. The king's intention became known, and it was necessary that the said king should not go unpunished for what he did and for the evil counsel he took (p282).

... Malacca is surrounded by Muhammedans who cannot be friends with us unless Malacca is strong, and the Moors will be unfaithful to us except by force, because they are always on the look-out, and when they see any part exposed they shoot at it (p286).

There is a sense too in which Pires considers Portuguese (and therefore Christian) triumph inevitable: *the truth is that Muhammed will be destroyed, and destroyed he cannot help but be* (p286). Indeed, it would also seem that he sees Christian progress as a reversal of history. *'Just as the Moors used to go on conquering kingdoms, they are now losing them'* (p57).

Negative Attitudes
At the same time, Pires also reports Muslim attitudes, particularly as they related to these European, Portuguese Christian conquerors. In talking about the conquest of Malacca the king there is reported to have said, ' *...I know as you know that they go about conquering the world and destroying and blotting out the name of our Holy Prophet'* (p256) .

---

[4] When the Portuguese attacked Malacca they were confronted by a fleet of ships from many of the surrounding Muslim kingdoms. Many, though not all of these rulers, had adopted Islam. Because of the considerable international trading and inter-relationships through marriage, most of the Muslim rulers sided with the King of Malacca with the aim of stemming both the progress of Christianity and Portuguese involvement in trade.

[5] A people group of South East Asia

In terms of this Christian progress, Pires suggested that it was causing some fear and groaning, especially as they were 'see[ing] their wealth fading away'.

Given his background it is not surprising that Pires records negative attitudes towards Muhammedans or Moors, as he calls them, whenever he found them. He admits that the only reason he included some material on Persia was, he said *because it is opposed to Muhammed* (p21). That is, Pires recognised the distinction and the ill-feeling that existed even then between the followers of Muhammed (Sunnis) and the followers of Ali (Shi'ites). Yet, commenting on Ceylon and its people he notes, *They are ill-disposed towards the Moors and worse towards us* (p87). Similarly of Siam he writes: *There are very few Moors in Siam. The Siamese do not like them* (p103) and apparently the people of Cochin China were not friendly to the Moors (p114) either. Interestingly Pires also suggests that the Chinese fear the Malay and the Javanese both of whom Pires portrays as being Moors.

So not surprisingly when writing about some of the kingdoms located in the Indonesian archipelago he made these comments:

> *The kingdom of Sunda [located on the island of Java] does not allow Moors in it, except for a few, because it is feared that with their cunning they may do there what has been done in Java; because the Moors are cunning and they make themselves masters of countries by cunning, because apparently they have no power* (p173).

The Advancement of Islam

One of the interesting aspects of Pires' *Suma* is that indirectly he records the advance of Islam throughout the area. In doing so he often comments on their mode of advancement.

> *Pase [located on the Island of Sumatra] used to have heathen kings, and it must be a hundred and sixty years now since the said kings were worn out by the cunning of the merchant Moors there were in the kingdom of Pase, and the said Moors held the sea coast and they made a Moorish king of the Bengalee caste, and from that time until now the kings of Pase have always been Moors; except that up till now they been unable to convert the people of the interior; and yet in these kingdoms there are in the island of Sumatra, those on the sea coast are all Moors on the side of the Malacca Channel, and those*

who are not Moors are being made so every day, and no heathen among them is held in any esteem unless he is a merchant (p143).

Not surprisingly when talking about the Arab traders, Pires notes (p174) that they

> ... flourished so greatly that Muhammed and his followers determined to introduce their doctrines in the sea-coasts of Java [together] with merchandise.
>
> Now I will begin to tell of the Muhammedan pates who are on the sea coast, who are powerful in Java and have all the trade because they are lords of the junks and people.

Similarly of the king of Achin [present day Aceh] he writes *This king is a Moor, a knightly man among his neighbours. He uses piracy when he sees an opportunity* (p137).

A little further on he notes:
> At the time when there were heathens along the sea coast of Java, many merchants used to come, Parsees, Arabs, Gujaratees [India], Bengalees, Malay and other nationalities, there being Moors among them. They began to trade in the country and grow rich. They succeeded in the way of making mosques, and mollahs[6] came from outside, so that they came in such growing numbers that the sons of these said Moors were already Javanese and rich, for they had been in these parts for about seventy years. In some places the heathen Javanese lords themselves turned Muhammedan, and these mollahs and the merchant Moors took possession of these places. Others had a way of fortifying the places where they lived, and they took people of their own who sailed in their junks, and they killed the Javanese lords and made themselves lords; and in this way they made themselves masters of the sea coast and took over trade and power in Java (p182).

Yet there were other ways Pires notes that Islam grew.

> And the heathens do not mind being married to Moorish women, because it is the custom here, and the Moors are better pleased to

---

[6] This term generally refers to the leader of a mosque. In other instances it refers to a person who has had training in the Qur'an and Islamic studies.

marry their women to heathens than for themselves to marry heathen women as they make their husbands Moors. This is the custom in these countries (p243).

In conclusion
As he journeyed Pires encountered Islam. Whenever he did, he saw it through the eye of a Portuguese Catholic whose very land had been won out of Moorish rule. Not surprisingly, Pires records what he experienced through the lens of the underlying worldview of his time towards the Moors. Was he surprised to encounter them there? He doesn't say but he certainly was keen to see the growth of Catholic influence.

Australia:
The Changing Religious Profile Down Under

Peter Riddell
Vice Principal (Academic)

Melbourne School of Theology

Australia holds a national census every five years, which has included a question about religious affiliation for several decades. Because of the vast amount of religious data assembled in this way, it is a relatively easy task to track the changing religious profile of the country over the last forty years.

In 1971, of a total population of 12.75 million, just over 86% identified themselves as Christian. Of this imposing majority, some 31% were Anglican, with Catholics coming in a close second at 27%. Other religions represented less than 1% of the population. Forty years ago, just under seven percent of Australians declared themselves to have no religion, while a similar number chose not to answer the question.

The most recent census in Australia, from June 2011, tells a very different story. Detailed figures are now available and paint a portrait of the prototypical western multicultural state.

There are four key messages to emerge from the most recent census figures. The first is that Christianity is both declining and is being significantly reshaped. The proportion of Australians declaring themselves to be Christians has slipped to 61% from the heady days of 1971. Within that figure, Catholics have benefited from immigration to outstrip the Anglican Church of Australia, which is suffering irreversible decline. One in four Australians is now Catholic, while the proportion of Anglicans, at 17%, is barely half that of 1971. So although once the statements of Anglican archbishops and bishops were taken as representing the voice of Christians in the media, today news media reports of significant Christian festivals such as Easter and Christmas tend to report first on Catholic activities and then on Anglican, followed by the plethora of other churches.

The second clear message to emerge from the 2011 census is the explosion in numbers of people declaring they have "No religion". Almost as many Australians opted to declare for 'no religion' as those identifying themselves as Catholics. Looking at it another way, the two largest groups declaring a position on religion in Australia are Catholics and Atheists. In addition to those declaring 'no religion', a further 9% chose not to answer the religious affiliation question.

The third message to emerge from the latest census figures is the ever expanding number of Australians identifying with non-Christian religions. Of the roughly 7% who do so, the largest group are Buddhists (2.5%), closely followed by Muslims (2.2%). But the fastest growing religion is Hinduism, with its numbers almost doubling between 2006 and 2011, largely reflecting the surge in immigration from India. So the skyline of Australia's cities, and to some extent towns, is being increasingly dotted by Muslim minarets, Hindu and Buddhist temples and pagodas, and Sikh gurdwaras.

Of course, census figures are not only useful for providing a synchronic picture of society at a given point in time, but can also help greatly with looking into the future. It is in this area that an important fourth message can be discerned.

In the ten year period between the 2001 and 2011 censuses, there was a marked decline in the numbers of adherents aged 1-14 for Catholics, Anglicans, Presbyterians and other Reformed Christian groups. In contrast, significant increases in this age group are recorded for Buddhists, Muslims and Hindus. In other words, the main Christian groups are ageing while other religions are growing among the youth.

This has clear ramifications for the future. Australians can expect future censuses to show a redrawing of the religious map in the country, with Christianity representing an ever decreasing proportion and adherents of other religions, or no religion, claiming an increasing voice in public discourse about matters of faith.

The 21st century will usher in huge social changes in Australia, not least in the area of religious affiliation. In this, Australia is little different from other Western countries, where similar trends have been in evidence for some time. Historical distinctions between West and East, North and South, are likely to become much more blurred in the decades to come.

Reflections

Islamic "Peace Conference" in Melbourne

Bernie Power
Islamics Lecturer

Melbourne School of Theology

It seemed like too good an opportunity to miss. Up to 20,000 Muslims gathering in the Melbourne Showgrounds for a three-day 'Peace Conference' in March, 2013! It coincided with an MST course "Christian Ministry in Islamic Contexts", so the timing was perfect. We'd be there! It would give us an opportunity to put into practice some of the theory we had been learning about how engage with Muslims.

Most of our MST class went along to the Conference, and we were joined over the weekend by a number of current and former MST students and others who are interested in Muslim outreach. The conference organisers prevented us from having a stall to sell or give away Christian literature including Bibles and New Testaments. They said they could not guarantee our safety from radical Muslims inside the Showgrounds. But that did not stop us from witnessing about Jesus – it just spread us out a lot more throughout the crowds. Over the weekend, about 60 Christians came to the Conference. We found Muslim people very willing to talk about spiritual issues. Hundreds of deep conversations took place. However the conference organisers were not too happy. The conference had been designed for *da'wa*, the propagation of the Islamic message to non-Muslims, but in fact the reverse was happening. Most of the non-Muslims who came were Christians, who were actively sharing their faith. Sometimes conference officials would intervene in our discussions, telling Muslims not to speak with us. Security personnel escorted six of our team out of the Showgrounds after Christian literature was given to Muslims. But the sharing continued through others.

The numbers did not reach the expectations of the conference organisers. Large meeting rooms had thousands of empty chairs, and some meetings were cancelled. The two main speakers were not present. A Saudi sheikh did not apply for a visa after it was revealed that he had called Jews "the scum of the earth", "rats" and "pigs" and called for their annihilation. Another sheikh, from Kuwait, came but fell sick and was unable to attend the conference.

On Sunday, hostile anti-Islamic protestors gathered outside the Showground gates holding posters calling for "No Mosques" and "No Shari'a law". We asked police permission to hold an alternative demonstration outside. Our banner, designed by an MST student, read: "Jesus loves Muslims. So do we." When we told the Muslim reception staff what we were going to do, they shook our hands vigorously and said 'Thank you'. We held it up outside the Showground gates, as we would not be permitted to do so inside, and the Muslim reception personnel came out to take pictures. One said: "I'm emailing this to my mother." They then joined us in the photos.

The banner was an important gesture. It balanced the words of truth and portions of Scripture that were being shared inside the conference, with a practical statement and demonstration of the love of Christ "outside the walls."

Ministry to Muslim Women
Report on a Seminar conducted by Dr Moyra Dale on *Caring and Sharing with Muslim Women*

On Monday 17th March, 2014 at the Melbourne College of Theology, Dr Moyra Dale, CSIOF Adjunct Research Fellow and member of the CSIOF Advisory Group conducted a seminar on 'Caring and Sharing with Muslim Women'. About 18 ladies each having varying degrees of contact with Muslim women were involved in the interactive program. Moyra opened the seminar by having the gathered group reflect on the distinctive situation of Muslim women and the fact that they are under-represented among Muslims who have come to faith in Christ.

The result of that interaction was the recognition that ministry to Muslim women calls for its own methodology – a methodology that is different from what is currently being taught and practiced. This is a reflection, no doubt, of the male domination of both current practice and theory. However, that position is being brought into question. At least one mission organisation has established a focus on women's ministry. The focus of the seminar was indeed to highlight the distinctive nature of ministry to women living within an Islamic context.

Part of that distinctiveness, Moyra demonstrated, relates to the views of women within Islam: These include the attitude to women which places most of them in hell and considers that they have no sense. Other factors include their position within society, their lack of education and knowledge of the Qur'an and even their limited ability to practice their religion.

Moyra also focused on a significant issue for women from a Muslim background – the question of 'baraka'. While the word has the sense of blessing it also incorporates the idea of power and the need to be able to survive within one's context and live life. In order to do that, Moyra had each of the groups consider the Biblical concept of blessing and cursing and then went on to speak of the importance of offering a 'blessing' especially in difficult situations.

In considering case studies of women who had come to faith in Christ, each group was forced to consider the challenge presented by the uniqueness of each woman's situation. The question of fostering fellowship and facilitating discipleship were the underlying issues in considering those particular case studies.

Each of the ladies who gathered expressed their appreciation of the session and their interest in having a follow-up session. Many were grateful for the new insights that were gained.

Dr Ruth Nicholls
Adjunct Research Fellow
CSIOF | MST

Leonard Buck Lecture 2014

The Leonard Buck Lecture is named after the great missionary statesman and founder of many missionary ventures, the late Mr Leonard Buck AO.

Veiled: Muslim Women and Mission Today[1]
Do Muslim women need saving?

Dr Cathy *

The image of the veiled woman is used for many different reasons. It conjures up ideas of poverty, inequality, being downtrodden and uneducated, marginalisation, violence and abuse. It was the image used to justify the war on terrorism. Laura Bush, wife of then President George Bush, famously said, about Afghanistan: "The fight against terrorism is also a fight for the rights and dignity of women."

So what about mission today? The veiled woman is still symbolic; the image used often to portray the Muslim world. However, particular definitions of contextualisation have led to assumptions that say

> *"Muslim women are too often left out of strategic church planting due to... .a 'gender-blind missiology.'"*

the great commission is best fulfilled by reaching men first, and the women will follow. American mission leader Fran Love stated in her famous 1996 journal article: "Muslim women are too often left out of strategic church planting due to ... a 'gender-blind missiology.'" This mission theory states that missionaries need first of all to influence heads of households and leaders who will in turn influence their families and those under their authority. While based on conventional wisdom . . . it is an incomplete perspective both for biblical and practical reasons." So, despite the symbolic images of the veiled woman in

> *... mission is veiling Muslims to the good news.*

---

[1] First printed in the *MST Ambassador*, issue 218, Spring 2014 and reprinted here with permission

mission among Muslims, mission is veiling Muslims to the good news.

The story,
In 1852 Mrs McKenzie, wife of an East India Company merchant, and Lady Mary Kinnaird, wife of a London banker, established the organisation that today is Interserve. They recognised that women, secluded in the zenanas of India (the women's area of the home), were hidden from the gospel and from education and health care. A deliberate and intentional engagement, challenging the prevailing cultural hegemony, took education and health in the name of Jesus to women who were otherwise marginalised. These beginnings of Interserve demonstrate the imperative of intentionality in including women as recipients of the gospel; made in the image of God, worthy of the whole gospel.

Reaching Muslim women is challenging. The physical veil can make women appear inaccessible. Returning to live in Egypt in 2008, each time I walked on the street I sensed I was withdrawing. I had lived there before, and in many ways it was home. I realised I was reacting to the fully veiled women whose numbers had grown over the years. It is hard to connect with women who seemed invisible to me.

What is 'accessibility' in mission, particularly in mission to Muslim women? Strategy often defines accessibility. Many hours were spent sitting drinking chai in staff rooms, the girls' rooms, and my room at the college where I worked in South Asia. I learned about life, the practical challenges and emotional pressures. I attended life events, laughed, cried and prayed through the everyday and the catastrophes. I learned to do life with the girls, staff and families of both. How accessible were they? If I was willing to do life with them they were absolutely accessible. Maybe it is our strategies that make Muslim women inaccessible.

Unveiling Muslim Women in our strategies
Anthropologists would be horrified at the use of imagery of unveiling. I wish to redeem that imagery by reminding us that the veil that separated us from God

> ... *in Christ the veil for Muslim women is also torn.*

was torn when Jesus died, and in Christ that veil for Muslim women is also torn. Our strategies should not separate them from an encounter with the One God.

The evidence that Muslim communities are best reached by concentrating efforts on the male family and community heads is contested. Concerns are that this focus is seeing a fellowship of believers from a Muslim background who are almost solely male. This is not surprising. The view of women is often so low that the chance of faith going along kinship lines is limited. One male believer from a Muslim background (a 'BMB') in the Middle East, with a recognised ministry in music, said he did not share his faith with his wife because she was 'just an illiterate village woman'.

Women following Jesus
Women from a Muslim background choose to follow Jesus for reasons that are often very different to those of men. They are embracing the journey with Jesus from places of need, brokenness, marginalisation, encounter, and revelation. Women need an encounter with Jesus, and truth that transforms the reality of today, giving security for tomorrow. They respond to Jesus when their felt needs are met as they experience truth. Women are attracted to Jesus because of the way he treated women.

There is also the question of identity. Women find it more difficult to define their identity as followers of Jesus in a Muslim context because they carry within their 'self' all that it means to be a good Muslim wife, daughter, mother, and woman. Their identity is tied to their family and social relationships. The system of honour and shame inscribed on Muslim women's bodies is an important reason why more men than women are coming to faith and visible in BMB fellowships. The construction of alternative communities, places of belonging, and identity in Christ are important in the journey of Muslim women with Jesus.

One woman's story
It started with a dream, a man in white coming and speaking to her. He told her that she should follow the way. Actually she had no idea what that meant. Then one day as she was watching television she saw a program and in it was the man who had spoken to her in her dream. Fatima had stumbled on a Christian satellite television program. She called the number they gave and began a journey to 'follow the way'. She is the first in her family to follow Jesus, but is

beginning to influence and shape her children. Maybe they will be the next generation of those who also follow Jesus.

Jesus set us an example by reaching out to women, breaking with tradition and cultural norms, intentionally seeking women out, and giving them dignity and hope. Mission needs to follow his example today.

To learn more of what God is doing, or to enable work among Muslim women to grow please contact Melbourne School of Theology, Centre for the Study of Islam and Other Faiths or Interserve.

This article is based on the 2014 Annual Leonard Buck Lecture, delivered by Dr Cathy* on 17 July, which tackled the important topic of Muslim women in modern mission strategies.

* Surname withheld to protect security.

Zorro, Goldilocks and Jesus

Mike Druber
Bachelor of Theology student

Melbourne School of Theology

I was reminded of the old Zorro movies as I attended a Forum recently, headed **'Jesus: Prophet, Messiah, God?'**

In the movies there was always a moment where the Spanish Dons were so close to discovering Zorro's true identity that it seemed all but assured that it would happen. Then, of course, came a rush of Zorro impersonators and the revelation that was all but assured was once again a mystery.

The Forum in July, hosted by City Bible Forum in conjunction with CrossCulture Church of Christ, attempted to 'unmask' the man called Jesus, posing the question whether he was a Prophet, the Messiah or God. The speakers at the Forum were:

- Shahir Naga: a Muslim and founder of the website 1GOD.com.au

- Steve Katsaras: a Unitarian minister and founder of Red Words Church, and

- Dr Bernie Power: a Trinitarian from Melbourne School of Theology.

Each speaker was given an eight minute window to present their view on the 'nature' of Jesus. The remainder of the forum was then an interactive question time, with brief closing statements from each speaker. It was not surprising that even after the forum closed there were still many questions left unanswered. They presented their views intelligently and respectfully and, for the most part, also clearly and concisely. No-one would be in doubt that each man had a very different view about Jesus.

Steve, who presented Jesus as a non-divine Messiah, clearly knew his material well, showing he had committed considerable time to preparation. However the use of overly academic language in his presentation limited his audience somewhat. Even though his conclusions were clear, it was hard to follow the line of argument objectively.

Shahir, on the other hand, presented a prophetic Jesus focusing particular attention on the nature of God as a single personality. Shahir illustrated his points from both the Qur'an and the Bible to reinforce his arguments. It was easier to follow his thinking and more appropriate language for the audience at the forum; however it would have been helpful to hear him speak in more depth on his points with broader citations to reinforce them.

The final speaker was MST's Dr Bernie Power, presenting Jesus as a divine part of a Trinitarian God. In many ways Bernie's presentation was the simplest of the three, keeping the language uncomplicated and using basic illustrations. His points were given strength by the associated material showing the breadth of research behind each of his points.

While each speaker presented quite clearly, listening at times felt a little like Goldilocks trying out the three bears' beds.

Was the forum a success? Yes, I think so. It succeeded in providing an open safe and encouraging environment where people of all faiths and backgrounds could come to hear and discuss big faith questions. A wonderful turnout on the night exceeded organisers' expectations and packed out the room. The fact that many approached the speakers after the forum to continue their enquiry was proof that the views expounded were not only heard but resonated with the audience.

As a Christian, I believe it also worked to show that the Jesus of the Bible is relevant for all people today. I would encourage you to watch the Forum, posted on City Bible Forum Melbourne's YouTube channel.

Let's keep these conversations going with our friends and colleagues, keep the question of 'Who Jesus is' on the agenda and remember that the word of God is a living word which does not go out in vain.

Sharing Christianity with Muslims
and Melbourne's Multicultural mix in Bourke Street Mall

Bernie Power
Lecturer in Islam and Missiology,

Melbourne School of Theology

It was a cold Saturday morning in the midst of Melbourne's winter. A fundamentalist Muslim group advocating Shari'a law in Australia had a table, just 20 metres away, and MST's fearless Missiologist Dr Bernie Power and a team of nearly 20 evangelists, including some born in Egypt, Lebanon and Iraq, Malaysia, Indonesia and the Philippines, dared to set up colourful banners proclaiming "We are Christians, Sharing Jesus, and engaging with Islam".

For over a year the Muslim book table has been distributing leaflets and proclaiming the message of Islam in Melbourne's Bourke Street Mall. A group of Arab Christians wanted to respond. "We felt that the Muslims had had a fair go and that we needed to give the Christian alternative," they said.

> A young Iranian man said: *"You would be put in prison for doing this in my country. But I'm glad you're here – I'm a Christian!"*

According to Dr Power, this Muslim group, which represents the more fundamentalist end of the Islamic community, is calling for the implementation of Shari'a law in Australia, and takes a polemical view towards Christianity. Its publications challenge the reliability of the Bible and deny the divine sonship of Christ and the Trinity.

Just 20 metres away, however, stood a Christian table with large banners proclaiming: *'Jesus loves Muslims. So do we.'* and *'We are Christians, Sharing Jesus, and engaging with Islam.'* The Christian literature includes New Testaments, Gospels and tracts in English, Arabic, Chinese and Indonesian. There is also a range of pamphlets responding to Islamic issues such as 'Was Muhammad sinless?',

'Has the Bible been corrupted?' and 'How to explain the Trinity to Muslims'.

The team of evangelists stood on the four corners of Bourke and Swanston streets, giving away a pamphlet contrasting Jesus and Muhammad and talking with people who were interested and, over the five hours, had dozens of significant conversations. The gospel was shared with people from Melbourne's multicultural mix - from Saudi Arabia, Somalia, Turkey and many other places.

A young Iranian man said: "You would be put in prison for doing this in my country. But I'm glad you're here – I'm a Christian!" The Muslim group was not so happy to see the team and initially moved their table away, but later returned to video the team's activities. They then left early.

Many passers-by stopped to commend the team: "We need to have some Christians here." A young Chinese woman came up to the table to say: "I'm getting baptised tomorrow – I'm sooo excited!" Two women came from the PlanetShakers conference: "Would you please pray for us?" The team prayed for several other people as well for various matters.

At a time when Christians are often being forced out of the public arena, it is good to have a clear and open presence in the city. The team assembles on Saturdays from 10 am to 4 pm and welcomes volunteers.

'Talking Past Each Other':
Shumack joins CSIOF

Well-known Sydney-based writer, academic and itinerant teacher on engaging Muslims, Dr Richard Shumack, will be taking over as Director of MST's Centre for the Study of Islam and Other Faiths (CSIOF) in February 2015. We spoke to Richard to discover what motivates him.

Richard says that one of the biggest problems for Christians wanting to engage Muslims is they so often 'talk past each other'. "Quite simply, we answer questions the other is simply not asking," he said.

Richard completed his PhD research at the National Centre for Excellence in Islamic Studies at the University of Melbourne. Richard's research examined the philosophy of present-day Muslims, particularly their epistemology, which asks the question "How do we know what we know?" (or "Why do we believe what we believe?"). His thesis focused on certainty and doubt, in particular the arguments and writings of Muslims philosophers, both traditional and Western.

"Most modern Muslims, even many Western Muslim intellectuals or academics, have a dualistic worldview, which recognizes two completely different sorts of knowledge. The first, and most important, sort is *divine revelation*. This is taken to consist of the Qur'an and the traditions of Muhammad. It is assumed to be unquestionably true. The second sort is *human empirical knowledge* which recognizes the need for reason and evidence. This framework limits the capacity of Muslims to examine their faith."

When asked why he chose a secular university like Melbourne University rather than a Christian school of theology (like MST) to complete his PhD, Richard said he wanted to really get inside how Muslims thought and wanted to learn from, and be assessed by, the best qualified Muslim philosophers and academics he could find. Richard says this has opened doors to him that simply would not be opened if he had studied at a seminary or Christian institution.

"Christians need to understand that Muslims have an unwavering confidence that their beliefs are true. The problem is that because most of their beliefs are unexamined this confidence is unwarranted."

"There is a saying in Islam, 'Kaffirs (or 'Infidels') ask questions'. Even for professional Muslim philosophers there are multiple 'no go' zones," he said.

Richard says his real passion is not Islam as a religio-political system but to understand deeply the Muslim mindset. He says his PhD research was "merely a means to an end."

"The original motivation for me was to understand Somalis. If you want to reach out and connect with Somalis, a very unreached people group, you need to understand Islam," he said.

After training originally at Moore College in Sydney and working in the Blue Mountains, Richard moved to Melbourne originally to work alongside Dr Peter Adam, then Vicar of St Jude's (Anglican) Community Church in Carlton, to head up a church planting team in their 'Estates Ministry'. He spent 12 years working with and reaching out to thousands of people on the Carlton Housing Estate, including many refugees and recent migrants from Somalia and other countries in the Horn of Africa.

"My calling and passion is not first and foremost to Muslims or necessarily to Academia but to sharing the gospel with unreached

Richard's book entitled *'The Wisdom of Islam and the Foolishness of Christianity'* was launched at the conclusion of the Leonard Buck Lecture on the 17th July, 2014 at the Melbourne School of Theology.

It is a philosophical apologetic to Western Muslims, dealing with the nine key objections that Muslims level at Christianity.

Richard noted that it is a direct response to the book *'The Qur'an and the Secular Mind'* by Pakistani-born Muslim philosopher, Dr Shabbir Akhtar, who lives and works in Oxford UK.

A review of his book appears in the book review section.

people groups. And it so happens that the vast majority of unreached people, over 1 billion in fact, are Muslims."

As part of his research, Richard has studied Arabic, having spent time living in Egypt with his wife Judy and four children before starting his PhD. He says the main reason he's keen to join MST's CSIOF is that it is one of the key Institutions in the world, and the leading institution in the Southern Hemisphere, seeking to understand Islam and the Muslim mindset from a Christian worldview.

"I can't promise I'll be a great administrator as a Board member but I am keen to do all I can to promote Christian understanding of Islam, especially through supervising hands-on research in the MST Postgraduate program," he said.

Richard is also a research fellow and regular writer for the *Centre of Public Christianity* (CPX) in Sydney. He is also employed by Ravi Zacharias International Ministries (RZIM) to coordinate global research engaging Islam. He was previously engaged by MST to supervise and coordinate student placement field work, for a decade, ending in 2011.

Reviews

> Readers are invited to submit reviews of recent publications on the study of Islam and other faiths for possible inclusion in the CSIOF Bulletin.

The Makings of Indonesian Islam:
Orientalism and the Narration of a Sufi Past

MICHAEL LAFFAN. *The Makings of Indonesian Islam: Orientalism and the Narration of a Sufi Past*, 2013, 241 pp., notes, index, EAN 978–0691145303.

In this important study, Dr Michael Laffan of Princeton University sets out primarily to address how Islam was interpreted in colonial Indonesia, rather than subjecting Indonesian Islam itself to the microscope.

That said, the author does devote the first part of the book to key trends in Indonesian Islam between 1300 and the early 20th centuries. In the first three chapters, he challenges a number of scholarly dogmas, scrutinizing the traditional view of Sufism as the primary engine of conversion to Islam in Indonesia and finding inconclusive evidence for this view. He highlights the difficulty of tracking the Islamisation process in the archipelago. He argues that "Sufism was formally restricted to the regal elite, while adherence to the Shari'a was commended to their subjects" (24). He also places important emphasis on the emerging gravitational pull of Arab world centres of learning from the earliest period.

Of particular interest in the early chapters is the focus on the emergence of Islamic schools in different parts of the archipelago. Drawing on a literary source base including historical and theological materials as well as classical Malay hikayats, Laffan challenges "the antiquity of the pesantren and the ubiquity of the tariqa in earlier periods" (38). He points to an increasingly standardized path of Islamic learning from the 17th century, one which restricted abstruse philosophical treatises to an elect scholarly class. This sets the scene for a valuable discussion of "Reform and the widening Muslim sphere" in the 19th century. He surveys the much-studied Wahhabi movement in Arabia and the Padri movement in Sumatra, arguing that the latter was in fact less Wahhabi than reformed Shattari. He provides an impressive account of inter-Sufi rivalry and conflict during this period, and traces the increasing numbers of pilgrims going to the Hijaz, thereby reinforcing the growing influence of centres of Islamic thought from outside the region. Laffan concludes Part One of the book by observing importantly that far from Sufism being the antithesis of reform in Indonesia during the late 19th century, in fact certain expressions of Sufism, especially those tied to Mecca, had become key to religious reform.

In Part Two (chapters four to six), the author moves to colonial perceptions, including Christian perceptions, of Islam. He begins with some very useful perspectives on early views of Islam by the first Dutch to reach the region, carrying forward Karel Steenbrink's important research in this area (*Dutch Colonialism and Indonesian Islam: Contacts and Conflicts 1596-1950*, Amsterdam & NY: Editions Rodopi B.V.; 2nd Revised edition 2006). Laffan trawls the archives of early letters and other correspondence between early Dutch missionaries and officials, including Georg Rumph and François Valentijn, signalling early what he presents as the biased perspectives of these early Dutch writers vis-à-vis Islam. The scene is thus set for one of the key themes of the book. He observes that the acquisition of Malay manuscripts by the early Dutch, including churchmen, contributed to the shaping of future Dutch-Muslim relations, concluding this fourth chapter with the key statement that "Islam ... was ... a familiar enemy now encountered in a new part of the world." (84)

In a fascinating chapter five, Laffan considers references to pesantrens in early 19th century Dutch records, emphasizing that the Dutch had "a text-based approach to Islam" (93). This fed into the establishment of various training schools for Dutch officials in Holland and later Batavia, as well as the emergence of scholarly journals from these institutes which provided a platform for publishing Dutch perspectives on Islam. Laffan portrays these early ventures in colonial official training as ineffectual especially in terms of understanding Islam and training officials to engage with it.

The author provides examples of how Dutch mission writers misunderstood key aspects of Islamic belief and practice. He writes: "Islam was a religion that they were determined to understand through the limited textual offerings available to them ... rather than through their experience of the field itself" (107). Placing particular attention on the prominent Dutch Christian writer L.W.C. Van Den Berg, Laffan observes that "Van Den Berg saw modern expressions of popular Sufism as mere superstition" and that he "was captive to his elite interlocutors." All was not lost in the writings of this Dutch scholar, however, because "[w]hatever his failings, Van Den Berg did signal that a sea change was in process in the pesantrens of Java" (118-119). Laffan concludes the second part of his book by observing that many missionaries "saw a chance for Christianising the natives given what appeared to them as the natives' weak understanding and practice of Islam ... If anything was clear by 1888, it was that Dutch knowledge of Islam was outdated and far too oriented towards texts above contexts" (121).

Part Three of Laffan's book (chapters seven to nine) is devoted to the seminal role of Dr Christiaan Snouck Hurgronje in moving on from early Dutch scholarly attitudes based on text-based normative approaches to the study of Islam. The reader is treated to a valuable sweep of the early life of Snouck, highlighting his original perspectives and outspoken critique from the very outset of his career. Snouck rejected previous Dutch views that Islam in the Netherlands East Indies (NEI) was a poor relation of the world faith (a view perpetrated especially by those with Christianising intentions, according to Laffan). Snouck was totally committed to a serious engagement with NEI Islam, through learning Malay and personally converting to Islam to enable a visit to Mecca in 1885 to encounter the faith as lived. Reiterating a core theme of his book, Laffan comments, "Trained in the field of religious studies, Snouck had a decided aversion to legalistic scholarship that prioritized text over context" (146). Nevertheless, the overriding purposes of this greater engagement for Snouck was to facilitate the colonial project; Laffan observes that Snouck was "a conscious servant of empire, albeit one who believed that he could play a part in the elevation of its subjects." Foreshadowing late 20th century western approaches, Snouck advocated "greater patience with, attention to, and even respect for Islam" (161).

Such a radical change was bound to arouse opposition. Laffan skilfully traces the rise and fall of Snouck Hurgronje's career in the NEI as Advisor on Native Affairs to the colonial government. Snouck rose to a position of great respect and prominence among Indonesian Muslims for his training and expertise in the Islamic sciences. He was highly critical in his writings of those Dutch scholars who impugned and derided expressions of Islam in the NEI. However, by the turn of the twentieth century Snouck's star was setting in the NEI, being suspected by some Dutch for his liberal views and by some Muslims as an infiltrator. He returned to the Netherlands in 1906, after a seventeen year stay, to take up a faculty position at the University of Leiden and to be closely involved in the ongoing training of Dutch colonial officials bound for the Indies.

Laffan devotes his last three chapters to the first half of the 20th century in the NEI, leading up to the Japanese occupation. This was a period of great change in Islam in the region, with a tide of reformism sweeping through the Indies. Laffan considers questions posed by individual Indies Muslims to scholars in Mecca and the resulting *fatwa* issued by expatriate Malay scholars such as Ahmad al-Fatani and Ahmad Khatib al-Minangkabawi. He also considers the influence of the reformist journal *Al-Imam* published in Singapore (1906-08), and its role as a conduit for modernist thinking coming from Cairo. Built into this discussion is the tension between some modernists and certain Sufis, with some other Sufi orders embracing reformism and playing a leading role in its dissemination.

Laffan also makes the interesting observation that by 1919 the British and Dutch had different approaches to the governance of their subjects in their respective Southeast Asian colonies: the former favoured traditional elites while the Dutch favoured modernist groups such as the Muhammadijah. Throughout the discussion in these final chapters, Laffan considers the ongoing role and influence of Snouck Hurgronje via the colonial officials whom he trained in Holland.

One of the great strengths of this book is also a weakness. It is erudite and encyclopaedic; however, at times the work is so dense as to be almost unreadable. This feature could have been assisted by the author paying more attention to the information flow for reader comfort. Moreover, a bibliography would have been helpful. The endnotes are at times impenetrable, making access to further sourcing difficult for students as well as for reviewers needing to check on the accuracy of detail. Moreover, there is some untidiness in endnotes with some first references to sources only including summary detail, which will hopefully be picked up in a second edition.

The main flaw in an otherwise excellent study is the good guy/bad guy dichotomy that appears periodically throughout the work, with a tone of authorial sarcasm at times verging on a sneer that ill befits such a serious scholarly study. The bad guys are the Dutch in general, but especially "the missionaries" who sought to "Christianize". On the one hand they are portrayed as a monolithic group who are bound to texts rather than context and who misunderstand diverse expressions of Islam in the Indies. They are seen as working hand in glove with the colonial authorities, "their protectors" (89). Yet at other places we catch glimpses of the odd missionary who isn't so bad after all (e.g. Poensen, 113), and we are also given hints of the kinds of tensions between missionary agencies and colonial authorities (101-103) that any serious study of Christian mission history has no difficulty identifying. Laffan might have benefited from maintaining a respectable distance from the scene he was painting rather than wearing his views so visibly in his references to missionary "propaganda" (101), "hawkish colonizers and Christianizers..." (203) and so forth.

Notwithstanding the above reservations, overall this is a significant and extremely valuable work. A key strength of the book is its presentation of the latest scholarly findings on a whole range of topics. For example, a lot has been written on the period covering 1300-1750, yet Laffan in his first chapter succeeds in creating a sense of freshness. He achieves this through his treatment of Hamzah Fansuri (10-12), a much studied figure for whom there is little new source information available. Having said that, Laffan is drawing a very long bow in his seeming acceptance of 1527 as the likely date for Hamzah's death and Mecca the place. That may represent the latest theory but it needs considerably more corroboration to be accepted as a given.

Laffan displays great erudition throughout the volume, such as his translation from the journal of Van Neck, as well as his detailed engagement with Snouck's diaries which record Snouck's human subject research with countless informants. The over-riding impression that is left with the reader of this volume is that Laffan is on top of all the relevant literature as well as being conversant with such diverse disciplines as history, theology, and mysticism in both Indonesia and the Arab world. This study will provide a benchmark for future scholarship for some time to come, and deservedly so.

Peter Riddell
Vice Principal (Academic)
Melbourne School of Theology

Islam and Christianity on the Edge
Talking Points in Christian-Muslim Relations into the 21st Century

JOHN AZUMAH AND PETER RIDDELL (EDS) Acorn Press, April 2013, 269pp, index, ISBN9780987132949 (pbk)

Everyone seems to know the old adage: "Those who don't know history are destined to repeat it" (Edmund Burke, (1729-1797)). I dare say it is also true that those who have no knowledge of what they are getting into are bound to make a mess of it! Indeed, unpreparedness will spoil the very best of intentions.

Every Christian who is passionate about engaging with Islam intellectually and/or with Muslims personally can probably recall an early experience when they, compelled by love, concern and passion for the glory of God, launched into dialogue only to be cut down and thoroughly humiliated. Some are so wounded by their experience they retreat or even retire. Others, awakened to the realisation of how fierce this spiritual battle is, get busy arming themselves in preparation for the next opportunity.

There are books on Islam and books on apologetics but nothing quite like *Islam and Christianity at the Edge* which unpacks the hottest topics in Muslim-Christian relations. Eminently readable, the papers collected in this volume will help any person who desires positive engagement with Islam and /or Muslims to equip themselves for the task.

This book, however, does much more than that. For not only does it lay a fertile foundation of knowledge, it also feeds sapling debates while planting fresh seeds of inquiry. One of the wonderful features of these papers is that they are non-arrogant. While respecting the complexity of their subject-matter, the writers present views that are expansive as distinct from definitive. Views are presented with conviction but without pressure -- leaving us with 'talking points' as distinct from doctrine. Readers will not agree with every position: indeed one expressed view almost made me faint! A talking point indeed!

As a religious liberty analyst who spends her days immersed in the horrors of religious repression and persecution, I was greatly encouraged by the diversity of Islamic thought presented. I was also shocked to discover (courtesy Thorneycroft) the differences between the English and Arabic translations of the Universal Islamic Declaration of Human Rights (Cairo 1981). It left me wondering: "Who is responsible for the meaning being lost in translation? Is this Western folly or Islamic deception? How widespread is this?" Derek Tidball's call to Western Christians, to "let go of Christendom" and realise that "a new day has dawned", excited me no end, for I share his view: "It is not a day to despair. Rather it is a day of new opportunity".

I am profoundly grateful to John Azumah and Peter Riddell for giving us this book. For through it many will be able to equip themselves to make the best of the opportunities God affords them.

Elizabeth Kendal is the author of *Turn Back the Battle: Isaiah Speaks to Christians Today* (Deror Books, Dec 2012)

Blogs: Religious Liberty Monitoring
Religious Liberty Prayer Bulletin
Web: www.elizabethkendal.com

Islam and Christianity on the Edge
Talking Points in Christian-Muslim Relations into the 21st Century

JOHN AZUMAH AND PETER RIDDELL (EDS) Acorn Press, April 2013, 269pp, index, ISBN9780987132949 (pbk)

This book is a timely contribution to the ongoing encounter between Christianity and Islam. John Azumah and Peter Riddell, editors of and contributors to this volume, are both well known for their balanced approach to discussion about Islam. The chapters from the different authors will help to forward conversation among Christians about ways of engaging with Islam, through the range of perspectives included.

The book deals with some controversial issues. Many of the chapters promise to be significant contributions to future directions of discussion. John Azumah brings a unique perspective to the debate on the Insider Movement in mission. The challenges of comparing the sources of Scriptures for both faiths are discussed. In addition the subject of Holy War is examined in the theological and historical contexts of both faiths, as well as for its different understandings among Muslims.

The title places Christianity and Islam in conversation: the middle part of the book focuses more on Islam and the Western world. It includes issues of epistemology and varying positions on human rights and gender. Hard questions are asked about stereotyping the 'other,' from both Western and Muslim perspectives and the place of Muslim populations with the west, in Australia and Europe, is viewed historically and ideologically.

The third section returns to the interaction between the Faiths, beginning with a noteworthy analysis of different Muslim and Christian positions and how they engage one another. An examination of the place of Christianity in Turkey is partnered by considered how Christianity and Islam interact with one another and in public space within Europe. Islamic sources are the base for a discussion of how Islam deals with those who want to leave it: and for an understanding of the call to a 'common word' (Qur'an

3:64) issued by Muslims to Christians. And the book concludes with a call to Christians to let their interaction with Islam and Muslims be guided by the Jesus Way.

Given the many areas of current debate covered, that of gender is a surprising omission. All the contributors to this book are Christian, and the editors note in their introduction that it will contribute to discussion among Christians about Islam. They have taken care to introduce a range of viewpoints, not all in agreement with one another. This variety, and the fact that all the issues discussed are also the subject of lively debate within the Muslim community, will ensure its relevance to a wide range of readership.

Dr Moyra Dale
Adjunct Research Fellow
CSIOF|MST

Turn Back the Battle
Isaiah Speaks to Christians Today

ELIZABETH KENDAL, Melbourne, Deror Books, 2012, 286pp, ISBN 978-0-9807223-6-9

Elizabeth Kendal has a passion and a concern. She is a spokeswoman for the persecuted church. She is aware of growing difficulties and dangers that lie ahead. She considers herself a religious freedom analyst and prayer advocate. In her book, *Turn Back the Battle, Isaiah Speaks to Christians Today,* Elizabeth, like the prophet in whose message she finds help and guidance, becomes a voice crying in the wilderness of Christian indifference amidst a world that is becoming increasingly hostile to Christ and his people.

In the face of that growing opposition Kendal explores parallels she has found in the early chapters of the prophecy of Isaiah. In those chapters she has discovered a way forward. In this book, she shares the lessons she has learnt, the inspirations and illuminations that will provide a way to 'turn back the battle'. Kendal is very aware that human strength and endeavour will not achieve God's righteous goals so each chapter ends with a prayer: a prayer of recognition of God's goodness; a confession of failure and of commitment and dependence. As a prayer advocate, Elizabeth knows and has experienced that prayer 'changes things' and provides others with an opportunity to share in that experience.

In the introduction Kendal paints the picture entitled 'You will have tribulation' (John 16:33) using examples from the vast resources of her religious freedom analysis. Kendal bases her sketch on the salient points of an editorial written by Gregory Copley. She then illustrates her discussion with examples taken from China, Iran and the UK as well as outlining her understanding of various world events and their impact on religious liberty.

In each of the following twelve chapters of her book, Kendal examines a section of Isaiah's prophecy eliciting from each passage the lesson she considers pertinent to the church and its individual members so that they can stand firm in the day of trouble. Kendal is not alone in her concerns for the future of the church and its believers. Others are also sounding a similar alarm. Kendal's cry is 'Listen church! Take heed! Learn from the prophet! Be equipped to turn back the battle!' Kendal shouts.

Does Kendal achieve her goal? From the endorsements at the front of the book, those readers have at least heard her cry. Sadly, for the most part, Isaiah's world did not hear his cry. Only in some cases was the battle 'turned'. I too have heard Kendal's impassioned pleas. The book pulsates with a sense of urgency and at times a sense of frustration, perhaps even a sense of hopelessness in that the message is falling on deaf ears. Yet, Kendal also presents a God who invites a deliberate trust and a committed obedience, who is also very aware of human frailty and sinfulness, yet a God who is capable of doing great things.

Dr Ruth Nicholls
Adjunct Research Fellow,
CSIOF/MST

The Wisdom of Islam and the Foolishness of Christianity
A Christian Response to Nine Objections to Christianity by Muslim Philosophers

RICHARD SHUMACK, Sydney, Island View Publishing, 2014, 240pp, notes, ISBN 978-0-9924997-0-9

The sacred texts of Islam have a clearly polemical edge vis-à-vis Christianity. Many different critiques of the Christian faith have been offered by Muslim scholars and popular writers down the ages. One angle of attack has been to portray Christianity as paradoxical, even nonsensical, in contrast with Islam, which such Muslim writers see as logical and rational.

In this important new study of Christian philosophical apologetics, Richard Shumack sets out to respond to such Muslim critiques, which he describes as "high on strong rhetoric, low on strong argument". He presents a range of Muslim scholarly statements which lay down the gauntlet to Christianity, and urges Christians to take such Muslim philosophical challenges seriously and to respond. In this book, Shumack leads the way by giving eloquent Christian responses to nine particular Muslim objections.

These challenges to Christianity will be familiar to Christians who engage in different ways with Muslims. However Shumack's responses are fresh and original, pointing to his gifts as a scholar and philosopher. He parries the Muslim critique of Christians who ask questions about their fundamental beliefs; in contrast certain fundamentals of Islamic belief – the status of Muhammad as prophet and Qur'an as divine word – are no-go areas for Muslims. He answers the common Muslim challenge to Christian belief in the inherent sinfulness of human nature. The problem of the Trinity makes an inevitable appearance in this book, and the author provides answers for Christians who will inevitably be faced by this challenge as they meet Muslims.

Also considered is the problem of incarnation – God coming as man – which bends Muslim minds, as seen in their polemical writing. The problem of the Cross makes an appearance, with Muslims rejecting the death of Christ at Calvary. Shumack's response is philosophically rigorous and logically watertight.

Shumack is the consummate apologist. His distinction between the Muslim legislative model and the Christian fellowship model of divine/human interaction is nothing short of brilliant. In his engagement with Muslim challenges to Christianity, Shumack shows his own excellent educational formation by referring widely to Muslim philosophical scholarly writings, including key individuals such as al-Faruqi, Said Nursi, Al-Attas, al-Ghazali and so forth.

It is also worth noting that this philosopher author does not fall into the trap of so many philosophical writers whose works become impenetrable and incomprehensible. On the contrary, Shumack's writing style is accessible and comprehensible from start to finish in this excellent volume.

Shumack is gracious and irenic, yet rigorous and to the point. He has been invited to debate his book with a leading Muslim scholar in Oxford in 2015 and this volume equips him well for that task. No doubt many Muslims will read this book, and Christians should too.

Dr Peter Riddell,
Vice Principal (Academic)
Melbourne School of Theology

Special Offer
CSIOF has a limited number of Richard Shumack's book available for purchase. The cost of the book is $15 but if requiring posting an extra $5 needs to be included. If desiring to purchase the book, contact the CSIOF.

CSIOF News and Activities

Postgraduate Research Seminars on Islam and related topics

2013

Design flaws in Pakistan's Blasphemy Laws, Qaiser Julius

Islamic Banking and Finance in Al-Andalus, Lincoln Loo

Muhammad as an Example of 'da'wa', Dennis Savelyev

The Abrahamic Fallacy, Mark Durie

2014

Basire & Frampton: The Cavalier Missionaries of the Seventeen Century, Andrew Lake

The Experience of Ahmadis and Christians under Pakistan's Blasphemy Laws, Qaiser Julius

Christians and Islamisation in Malaysia, Peter Riddell

The Spread of Islam in Somalia, Ken Okello

Voodoo Religion and Koranic Revelation, Mark Durie

A Critical Review of Theological Approaches to Islamisation, Ooi Chin Aik

GLOSSARY

Term	Description
Caliph	The successor to Muhammad as political and military ruler of the Islamic community
Dar al-Islam	The House of Islam; areas where Islam has political dominance
Dar al-Harb	The House of War; the rest of the world not under Islam
Da'wa	Mission
Dhimmi	"protected" non-Muslim communities (Second class citizens)
Durura	Necessity
Fasiq	Sinner
Hadith	Authoritative traditions of all that Muhammad said and did
Hajj	Pilgrimage (to Mecca)
Hijra	Migration
Huda	Guidance
Ijtihad	Process of legal deduction by which a scholar produces a legal opinion
Imam	(Sunni meaning) leader of congregational prayer in mosque as well as a community leader (Shia meaning) a person of spiritual authority and importance; also refers to a number of recognised leaders (General use) A recognised Muslim scholar
Jahiliyya	Paganism/ Ignorance
Jihad *Jehad*	Holy war; "a continuous and never-ending struggle waged on all fronts including political, economic, social, psychological, domestic, moral and spiritual." [Malite, p54]
Jinn	Demon/ spiritual being

Term	Description
Jizya	"Tax" if not converting to Islam
Kafir	Unbeliever/ disbeliever/ infidel
Maslaha	Public good
Mujaddid	Renewer of Islam
Mujahiddin	Holy warriors
Mu'min	Believer
Nur	Light
Saracens	Name Christians used for Muslims initially
Seerah	Biography of Muhammad
Shahada	Repeating "There is no God but God and Muhammad is his messenger"
Sunna	Way or example of Muhammad
Sura	Chapter of the Qur'an
Tafsirs	Qur'anic commentaries
Tahrif	Corruption, distortion (of text)
Taqlid	Imitation of judgements made by earlier scholars
Tawhid	Oneness of Allah (Sufi meaning) Oneness with Allah
Umma	One Muslim community worldwide
Zakat	Almsgiving at the mosque (Sufi meaning) totally giving oneself to Allah and to a Sufi brotherhood

Notes for Contributors

Submission requirements:

Manuscript

Papers should be 1000-1500 words, with a maximum of 1500. Papers with more than 1500 words will not be considered.

Submissions prepared in Microsoft Word format are preferred.

All papers are to be written in English, and an English transliteration given to any quotations or short phrases in original language.

Authors are advised to use gender inclusive and non-discriminatory language.

Any visuals should be integrated into the document, or sent separately as separate jpg or gif files with an explanation as to their position in the paper.

Footnotes should follow the style used in previous issues of the Bulletin. If footnotes are used, do not include a bibliography. When including a bibliography only cite works mentioned in the paper.

When quoting or referring to an internet site add the date on which the item was cited. For example www.reference cited dd/mm/yy. This is necessary as internet sites can change.

Submission

Papers to be considered for inclusion are to be submitted directly to the Editor.

Submissions are to be forwarded via electronic mail to csiof@mst.edu.au . If submitting within Australia; a hard copy must also be posted to CSIOF, PO Box 6257 Vermont Sth, Vic 3133.

A declaration that the submitted articles are your own work and that you've acknowledged the work/s of others used in the articles in the references, etc. must be included with any submission.

A covering letter that includes the authors' names, titles and affiliations, together with complete mailing addresses, including email, telephone and facsimile numbers should be attached to the paper.

Review of Submissions

All submissions will be sent to referees for anonymous recommendation.

The Editor holds the right to make editorial corrections to accepted submissions.

Copyright

The CSIOF Bulletin is published by the Melbourne School of Theology Press. The copyright for any published papers will remain with the author. MST publishes these papers on the following conditions:

- They do not appear elsewhere (including web pages) for 180 days from the date of publication in the CSIOF Bulletin.

- Whenever they are printed elsewhere (including web pages), the following notice will be included: "This article first appeared in the __ issue, date of the CSIOF Bulletin series".

The CSIOF\MST retains the right to use the paper in any of the CSIOF publications, whether reprint or in some electronic form (i.e. Online, CD-Rom, etc.).

The CSIOF\MST retains the right to use a portion or description of the paper with your name in our promotional material.

Authors are themselves responsible for obtaining permission to reproduce copyright material from other sources.

The author will be presented with one copy of the publication.

Disclaimer

The opinions and conclusions published in the CSIOF Bulletin series are those of the authors and do not necessarily represent the views of the Editor or the CSIOF. The CSIOF Bulletin serves purely as an information medium, to inform interested parties of religious trends, discussion and debates. The Bulletin does not intend in any way to actively promote hatred of any religion or its followers.

www.ingramcontent.com/pod-product-compliance
Lightning Source LLC
Chambersburg PA
CBHW072053290426
44110CB00014B/1668